LEADER'S GUIDE

Gary L. Ball-Kilbourne (Ph.D., Vanderbilt University) is the executive editor of adult publications in the Division of Church School Publications of The United Methodist Publishing House and of the General Board of Discipleship of The United Methodist Church. He has served as pastor of churches in North Dakota and West Virginia and is the writer of over twenty articles and curriculum resources.

JOURNEY THROUGH THE BIBLE: GENESIS. LEADER'S GUIDE. An official resource for The United Methodist Church prepared by the General Board of Discipleship through the division of Church School Publications and published by Cokesbury, a division of The United Methodist Publishing House; 201 Eighth Avenue, South; P. O. Box 801; Nashville, TN 37202. Printed in the United States of America.

Scripture quotations in this publication, unless otherwise indicated, are from the New Revised Standard Version of the Bible, copyright © by the Division of Christian Education of the National Council of the Churches of Christ in the United States of America, and are used by permission. All rights reserved.

For permission to reproduce any material in this publication, call 1-615-749-6421, or write to Cokesbury, Syndication–Permissions Office, 201 Eighth Avenue, South, P.O. Box 801, Nashville, TN 37202.

To order copies of this publication, call toll free 1-800-672-1789. Call Monday–Friday 7:30-5:00 Central Time or 8:30-4:30 Pacific Time. Use your Cokesbury account, American Express, Visa, Discover, or MasterCard.

© Copyright 1994. All rights reserved.

 **Cokesbury**

EDITORIAL TEAM

Dal Joon Won,
Editor

Norma L. Bates,
Assistant Editor

Linda O. Spicer,
Adult Department Assistant

DESIGN TEAM

Susan J. Scruggs,
Design Supervisor,
Cover Design

Ed Wynne,
Layout Designer

ADMINISTRATIVE STAFF

Duane A. Ewers,
Editor of Church School Publications

Dal Joon Won,
Managing Editor of Church School Publications

Gary L. Ball-Kilbourne,
Executive Editor of Adult Publications

09 10 11 12 13 – 18 17 16 15 14 13 12 11 10 9 8

THIS PUBLICATION IS PRINTED ON RECYCLED PAPER

CONTENTS

| Volume 1: Genesis | by Gary L. Ball-Kilbourne |

Introduction		2
Chapter 1	CREATION	3
Chapter 2	SIN	8
Chapter 3	FLOOD	13
Chapter 4	PRIDE AND CONFUSION	18
Chapter 5	COVENANT AND SOJOURN	23
Chapter 6	WILLFULNESS AND GRACE	28
Chapter 7	HOSPITALITY AND LAUGHTER	33
Chapter 8	SODOM AND GOMORRAH	38
Chapter 9	SACRIFICE	43
Chapter 10	ESAU AND JACOB	48
Chapter 11	JACOB AND GOD	53
Chapter 12	DREAMS	58
Chapter 13	RESTORATION	63
HOW TO CREATE EXCITEMENT FOR BIBLE STUDY		68
THE TORAH: THE BOOKS OF GOD'S COMMUNITY		70
MAP: THE ANCIENT NEAR EAST BEFORE THE EXODUS		Inside back cover

Introduction

The leader's guides provided for use with JOURNEY THROUGH THE BIBLE make the following assumptions:
- adults learn in different ways:
  —by reading
  —by listening to speakers
  —by working on projects
  —by drama and roleplay
  —by using their imaginations
  —by expressing themselves creatively
  —by teaching others
- the mix of persons in your group is different from that found in any other group.
- the length of the actual time you have for teaching in a session may vary from thirty minutes to ninety minutes.
- the physical place where your class meets is not exactly like the place where any other group or class meets.
- your teaching skills, experiences, and preferences are unlike anyone else's.

We encourage you to discover and develop the ways you can best use the information and learning ideas in this leader's guide with your particular class. To get started, we suggest you try following these steps:

1. Think and pray about your individual class members. Who are they? What are they like? Why are they involved in this particular Bible study class at this particular time in their lives? What seem to be their needs? How do you think they learn best?
2. Think and pray about your class members as a group. A group takes on a character that can be different from the particular characters of the individuals who make up that group. How do your class members interact? What do they enjoy doing together? What would help them become stronger as a group?
3. Keep in mind that you are teaching this class for the sake of the class members, in order to help them increase in their faithfulness as disciples of Jesus Christ. Teachers sometimes fall prey to the danger of teaching in ways that are easiest for themselves. The best teachers accept the discomfort of taking risks and stretching their teaching skills in order to focus on what will really help the class members learn and grow in their faith.
4. Read the chapter in the study book. Read the assigned Bible passages. Read the background Bible passages, if any. Work through the Dimension 1 questions in the study book. Make a list of any items you do not understand and need to research further using such tools as Bible dictionaries, concordances, Bible atlases, and commentaries. In other words, do your homework. Be prepared with your own knowledge about the Bible passages being studied by your class.
5. Read the chapter's material in the leader's guide. You might want to begin with the "Additional Bible Helps," found at the *end* of each chapter in the leader's guide. Then look at each learning idea in the "Learning Menu."
6. Spend some time with the "Learning Menu." Notice that the "Learning Menu" is organized around Dimensions 1, 2, and 3 in the study book. Recognizing that different adults and adult classes will learn best using different teaching/learning methods, in each of the three dimensions you will find
   —at least one learning idea that is primarily discussion-based;
   —at least one learning idea that begins with a method other than discussion, but which may lead into discussion.

   Make notes about which learning ideas will work best given the unique makeup and setting of your class.
7. Decide on a lesson plan: Which learning ideas will you lead the class members through when? What materials will you need? What other preparations do you need to make? How long do you plan to spend on a particular learning idea?
8. Many experienced teachers have found that they do better if they plan more than they actually use during a class session. They also know that their class members may become frustrated if they try to do too much during a class session. In other words
   —plan more than you can actually use. That way, you have back-up learning ideas in case something does not work well or something takes much less time than you thought.
   —don't try to do everything listed in the "Learning Menu." We have intentionally offered you much more than you can use in one class session.
   —be flexible while you teach. A good lesson plan is only a guide for your use as you teach people. Keep the focus on your class members, not your lesson plan.
9. After you teach, evaluate the class session. What worked well? What did not? What did you learn from your experience of teaching that will help you plan for the next class session?

May God's Spirit be upon you as you lead your class on their *Journey Through the Bible.*

Genesis 1:1–2:4a

LEARNING MENU
Keeping in mind the ways in which your class members learn best, as well as their needs and interests, choose at least one learning segment from each of the three Dimensions.

Dimension 1: What Does the Bible Say?

(A) Answer the questions in the study book.

The preferred method for working on Dimension 1 is to ask participants to complete the questions in advance of the class session. Then you may spend a short amount of time sharing and discussing answers briefly. The intent of Dimension 1 is to provide a quick way for persons to get into the Bible text itself. However, most of the class members' time should be spent on Dimensions 2 and 3.

If participants do not work on Dimension 1 questions beforehand, you may want to allow them a brief amount of time to read the recommended Bible passage and to answer Dimension 1 questions, either individually or in teams.

- Discussions of Dimension 1 questions might lead you in these directions:
  1. Creation takes place with this pattern:
     —God calls something into being by saying, "Let there be . . ."
     —That something comes into being.
     —Some details might be noted about the new something.
     —God sees that the newly created something is good.
  2. Several points might be noted about God's creation of humankind:
     —God intentionally creates humankind in God's own image.
     —God creates humankind to have "dominion" over other living creatures.
     —The initial creation of humankind included both male and female, apparently on an equal basis.
  3. The seventh day is a special day of holiness recognizing that God rested after creating all that is. For further information about the sabbath, you might draw the group's attention to the sidebar on "Sabbath" page 6 in the study book.

(B) Share information about the Book of Genesis.

- Note the sidebar, "How to Get More Out of Reading the Bible," on page 3 of the study book.

- Ask persons to locate any article in their Bible that introduces the Book of Genesis. These articles are often found at the beginning of Genesis, or class members may look in the table of contents.
- A few Bibles might not have any introductory articles. You may wish to have a few one-volume commentaries on the Bible for persons to use in this case.
- Ask persons to read their introductory article and to note up to three things they did not know before about the Book of Genesis.
- Share together what persons have learned from their reading.

Dimension 2: What Does the Bible Mean?

(C) Consider Creation from God's point of view.

Both of the stories about Creation in Genesis—the one in Genesis 1:1–2:4a as well as the one in Genesis 2:4b-24, are told in the third person from the perspective of an observer. (Wondering who might have been around to observe and describe how God created all there is may be an interesting question to ask but an impossible one to answer.)

- Ask persons to read the two Creation stories. Then invite them individually, or in groups of two or three, to come up with a retelling of the Creation story from God's perspective. In other words, tell the story of Creation as if God was telling it God's self. Persons or teams may find it helpful to write down notes for their stories on scratch paper.
- Allow time for sharing Creation stories.

(D) Experience a little bit of creating.

- You will need to have modeling clay, drawing tools, paper, scissors, paints, and other art resources. Depending on what you offer for use, you may also wish to have on hand facilities for washing up.
- Ask persons to use the art resources available to create something. It does not matter what they create. Just ask them to create something and to be able to share a little about why they created what they did.
- Discuss:
—What did it feel like to create something?
—How did you go about deciding what to create?
—How do you feel about what you created?

Be aware that many adults are not used to expressing themselves through art forms. A few may even consider this learning activity to be foolish or childish. Encourage them to be "good sports" and to try creating something anyway. Other members of your group may learn best through creative experiences that call them to do something with their hands and their feelings. The more-or-less rational discussions that many adults are used to provide only one way for adults to learn. Some adults learn better through other means.

(E) Take a closer look at the sabbath.

- Ask persons to read Genesis 2:1-3 as well as the sidebar on "Sabbath" on page 6 of the study book. They may also want to read Exodus 20:8-11 and Deuteronomy 5:12-15, which are the commandments in the Ten Commandments that institute the observance of the sabbath.
- You might also want to have Bible dictionaries and commentaries available for persons to do research on the topic of "Sabbath."
- Discuss such questions as:
—What is the sabbath?
—What seems to be the purpose or purposes of the sabbath?
—How do you observe the sabbath?
—How should Christians observe the sabbath?
—To what extent should persons who are neither Christians nor Jews be expected to observe the sabbath?

(F) Compare the two Creation stories.

- Invite persons to read the two stories of Creation found in Genesis 1:1–2:4a and Genesis 2:4b-24. They may also wish to look at the chart depicting "Two Tellings of Humanity's Origins," found on page 7 of the study book.
- Use the information presented in "More Than One Tradition" in the "Additional Bible Helps" on page 6 of this leader's guide.
- Discuss:
—What differences do you consider significant between these two stories of Creation?
—What similarities do you consider significant?
—If we only had the first story of Creation, as told in Genesis 1:1–2:4a, what would we be missing? For example, what does the second story tell us about the nature of God or of human beings that the first story does not?
—If we only had the second story, as told in Genesis 2:4b-24, what would we be missing?

(G) Learn what Creation tells us about God.

Note that the study book states that the first story of Creation is actually not so much about creation as it is about God.

- In teams of two or three persons, ask group members to read the Creation story told in Genesis 1:1–2:4a.

- Ask the teams to discuss these questions:
  1. What does the Creation story of Genesis 1:1–2:4a say or suggest to us about the nature of God?
  2. From a reading of this passage, what list of adjectives describing God can you make?
  3. What does your present experience of creation say or suggest to you about the nature of God?

Dimension 3: What Does the Bible Mean to Us?

(H) Play scientists and theologians.

- You will need to provide newsprint, markers, and masking tape for two teams to use.
- Read or summarize the material presented in "An Unnecessary Quarrel," on pages 7–8 of the study book.
- Ask persons to discuss what they think of the distinction made in the study book between "facts" and "truth."
- Divide the group into two teams: "Scientists" and "Theologians." Assign the "Scientists" the task of listing on newsprint as many scientific facts as they can agree on concerning the creation of the world and the universe. Assign the "Theologians" the task of listing on newsprint as many theological truths as they can agree on concerning the creation of the world and the universe.
- Ask the "Scientists" and "Theologians" to share their respective lists.
- Ask the "Scientists" to keep in their roles as scientists concerned with observable and experimentally provable facts. From within that role, what comments would they make about the list of theological truths developed by the "Theologians"?
- Ask the "Theologians" to keep in their roles as theologians concerned with discerning truths about God and about reality from God's perspective. From within that role, what comments would they make about the list of scientific facts developed by the "Scientists"?
- One of the acknowledged geniuses of our era is Stephen Hawking, who is Lucasian Professor of Mathematics at Cambridge University (the same academic position held by Sir Isaac Newton). Much of Professor Hawking's work has related to theoretical physics and the origins of the universe. The box in the next column contains a statement Professor Hawking made in an interview. Read it to the group and ask for their responses.

(I) Look at God's commands to newly created humanity.

Read or summarize the material contained in "Human Responsibilities," on pages 8–10 of the study book.

> "All that my work has shown is that you don't have to say that the way the universe began was the personal whim of God. But you still have the question: Why does the universe bother to exist? If you like, you can define God to be the answer to that question." (From *Black Holes and Baby Universes and Other Essays*, by Stephen Hawking; Bantam Books, 1993; page 173.)

Note that each of the two Creation stories contains a specific command from God to the newly created human beings. In Genesis 1:28, God commands humanity to "be fruitful and multiply, and fill the earth and subdue it; and have dominion over the fish of the sea and over the birds of the air and over every living thing that moves upon the earth." In Genesis 2:15, God places the first human in the garden in order "to till it and keep it."

- Ask the group—as a whole group, or as teams, or as individuals—to look at the commands God gives to humanity in Chapters 1 and 2 of Genesis.
- Discuss:
—Are all or parts of these commands still relevant to the human situation today?
—Does your understanding of the relevance of these commands change with the realization of the fact that when the Book of Genesis was written down in its present form, there were somewhat fewer than 200 million people on the entire earth? Today, the population of the earth exceeds 5.5 billion people.
—In what concrete ways might you as an individual fulfill these commands from God? What might you do as a class? What might you do as a congregation?

(J) Consider the limitations of human freedom.

- You will need plain sheets of 8½-by-11 paper and markers for each member of the group.
- If you have not already done so, read or summarize the material found in "Human Responsibilities" on pages 8–10 of the study book.
- Ask participants individually to read Chapters 1 and 2 of Genesis and to reflect upon the extent to which human beings are free to act and the extent to which their freedom is limited in various ways.
- Give the participants this task: They are individually to devise some kind of graphical depiction or representation of the extent to which human beings are free to act.
- Invite persons to share their graphical depictions and representations.
- Discuss:
—To what extent are human beings free to act? To what extent are they limited?
—In what ways do you personally feel limitations on your

freedom to act that arise from the Creation stories of Genesis?
—Are human beings free enough? Why, or why not?

(K) Imagine the image of God.

- You will need to provide scratch paper and a number of Bible concordances for this learning activity. One good, easily usable concordance is the *Concise Concordance to the New Revised Standard Version*, edited by John R. Kohlenberger III, Oxford University Press, 1993. Some individuals or churches may have access to versions of the Bible on computer, which may be used as concordances. One example is *QuickVerse for Windows*, Parsons Technology, 1992.
- Read or summarize the material presented in "The Image of God," pages 9–10 of the study book.
- Divide the class into teams, preferably providing each team with at least one copy of a Bible concordance.
- Tell class members that a Bible concordance is a useful tool for discovering where specific words are found in the Bible. Studying a word or group of words with the aid of a concordance can help us understand the contexts and various ways in which those words are used in different parts of the Bible. Concordances list alphabetically words found in the Bible. Under each word is a listing of each verse in which that word appears.
- Ask teams to use concordances to study the ways in which the word *image* is used at different points in the Bible.
- Once they locate places at which the word *image* appears, they should look up that verse in their Bible and read the surrounding verses to get a sense of the context of the verse. Then they should consider whether and in what ways that usage of the word *image* might bear upon an understanding of "the image of God" in Genesis 1:26-27.
- If concordances are not available, ask teams to consider how the following verses help them understand "the image of God" in Genesis 1:26-27:
  Genesis 5:3
  Genesis 9:6
  Acts 17:29
  2 Corinthians 3:18
  2 Corinthians 4:4
  Colossians 1:15
  Colossians 3:10
- Ask teams to report what they learned about "the image of God" from their study.
- Discuss: What do you think your understanding of "the image of God" tells you about the nature of God? About the nature of humanity?

Additional Bible Helps

More Than One Tradition
Many Bible scholars believe that several oral traditions lay behind the Book of Genesis (and the rest of the Old Testament) as we have it today. The Pentateuch (PEN-tuh-tyook)—or the five books of the Law (Genesis, Exodus, Leviticus, Numbers, and Deuteronomy)—was placed in its final form as we now read it sometime during the period of the Babylonian Exile and the Restoration to Israel in the fifth and sixth centuries before Christ.

These scholars believe on the basis of their research that the first Creation story found in Genesis 1:1–2:4a originated in a "Priestly" source that was written down after the destruction of Jerusalem in 587 B.C. This "Priestly" source is sometimes known as "P." The second Creation story that begins in Genesis 2:4b comes from an older source, probably written down in the southern region of Judah around 950 B.C. This old, Judean source is sometimes known as "J," after the usage of the name *Jahweh* (YAH-weh, also written as "Jehovah" or "Yahweh") as the primary name of God.

Scholars also identify at least two other sources in the Pentateuch: An older northern Israelite source from around 850 B.C., known sometimes as "E," because of the use of the name *Elohim* (EL-oh-him) for God; and a yet older source best viewed in the Book of Deuteronomy, dating from the religious reform of King Josiah in 621 B.C., sometimes known as "D," for "Deuteronomic" tradition.

Awareness of the presence of different sources in Genesis and in other books of the Bible will help us understand why the same story is often told more than once, sometimes from quite different perspectives. However, we should not be overly surprised that more than one source was drawn upon to put together Genesis and other books of the Bible. In our modern times, by comparison, our understanding of historic events is often shaped by the drastically differing perspectives of various historians.

Respecting the integrity of the different traditions of the Bible might cause us more work in studying, but it will also add to the richness and depth of our understanding of the biblical text. We should not try to force the two Creation stories to merge together into one supposedly comprehensive account. Instead, we should read each of the two stories separately, appreciating what each individually offers to teach us about God, about creation, about humanity, about ourselves.

(One good source for further information is *Understanding the Old Testament*, by Bernhard W. Anderson, fourth edition, Prentice-Hall, 1986, chapter 1.)

The Legend of the Angels' Debate Over Humanity
In the period of roughly A.D. 400–1200, Jewish rabbis collected interpretations and folk traditions relating to the Old

Testament. These stories often served the purpose of "filling in the gaps" left unfilled by the Bible itself. This collection of interpretations and folk traditions is known as *Midrash* (MID-rash), with the individual stories or comments known as *midrashim* (mid-RASH-im).

One such midrashim tells of a debate held by the angels in heaven over the relative wisdom of creating humanity:

"Whom did God speak to when saying 'Let us. . .'? Some rabbis say it was the ministering angels to whom God spoke and that there was some strong disagreement over whether the human should be created at all. The angel of love supported God's creation of the human because of all the acts of compassion that would enter the world through human beings. The angel of truth opposed the human because of the lies that humans would tell. The angel of righteousness was for the human, since humans would do many righteous deeds, but the angel of peace was against the human because humans would start wars. While the angels were arguing among themselves, God created the humans, male and female, and told the angels to be quiet: 'It's too late to argue; humans are a fact of life now.' " (Genesis Rabbah 8.4, from *The Storyteller's Companion to the Bible*, Volume One, "Genesis," edited by Michael E. Williams; Abingdon Press, 1991; page 29.)

2

Genesis 3:1-13

Sin

LEARNING MENU
Keeping in mind the ways in which your class members learn best, as well as their needs and interests, choose at least one learning segment from each of the three Dimensions.

Dimension 1: What Does the Bible Say?

(A) Answer the questions in the study book.

Continue to encourage your class members to read the Bible texts and study book material before class, as well as to answer the Dimension 1 questions ahead of time. However, if many persons still have not done so, allow a brief amount of time to read Genesis 2:15-17 and Genesis 3:1-24 and to write down answers to the Dimension 1 questions.
- Discussion of Dimension 1 questions might lead you in these directions:
    1. The short answer is that we do not really know why the first woman gave in to the serpent's temptation. The Bible text itself does not actually mention a specific motivation for eating the fruit of the [tree] of the knowledge of good and evil. One might speculate on the basis of Genesis 3:6 that she wanted the wisdom the fruit of the tree could impart, or that she was simply struck by the attractiveness of the fruit. On the basis of verse 4, one might speculate that she succumbed to the serpent's temptation to become "like God."
    2. Both the first man and the first woman blamed the influence of someone else. The first man blamed the first woman, while the first woman blamed the serpent. More discussion of the excuses and other actions of the first man and the first woman upon eating the fruit are given in the section on "Taking Sin Seriously," pages 15–16 of the study book.
    3. One can make a case that the real sin in this story had little to do with who ate what fruit. The real sin consists in the attempt of the first man and the first woman to place their own will before God's will. God had said not to eat of this particular fruit. A complete surrender to God's will would have acknowledged God's desire in this matter to be enough. The first humans decided they knew better than God, however; or at least they decided that they should place their own desires ahead of God's.

(B) Read the temptation story dramatically.

- Ask volunteers to read the parts of the serpent, the man, the woman, God, and a narrator.
- Allow a few moments for readers to look over Genesis 3, noting which parts are theirs. The narrator should prepare all portions not spoken within quotation marks.
- If your volunteers are so inclined, encourage them to block out actions to match what happens in the chapter.
- After the dramatic reading of Genesis 3, discuss:
—What did you notice during the dramatic reading of Genesis 3 that you had not noticed before?
—What did you notice about the character of the serpent? of the first woman? of the first man? of God?
—What were the conflicts in this drama?

Dimension 2:
What Does the Bible Mean?

(C) Look at the story from different points of view.

- Divide the class members into four teams.
- Assign each team one of the characters in this story: the serpent, the first woman, the first man, God.
- Ask each team to read Genesis 3 while focusing on the point of view of their assigned character. Each team should note the actions of its character, possible motivations, and the influence and effect of the actions of others upon the character.
- Provide time for each team to report its findings.
- Discuss:
—What did you learn from focusing on different points of view?
—What difference does it make to understanding this story if we think of God as the primary actor—as the main character—instead of assuming that the humans are the main characters?
—What do we learn about God?

(D) Convene a grand jury.

- Inform your class members that they are now being convened as a grand jury. Something terribly wrong has happened in the garden of Eden. All the evidence and testimony they have to go on can be found in Genesis 3. They should elect a jury foreperson and proceed to deliberate about who should be indicted for what crime. They should keep in mind that a grand jury does not determine guilt or innocence; it only determines whether enough evidence exists to say that a person should be tried for a crime.
- You may want to give your "grand jury" a time limit, such as ten or fifteen minutes (depending on what else you plan to do during your class time), for its deliberations.
- After deliberations, ask the jury foreperson to read the bill of indictment, if any.
- Allow time for participants to talk about their experience in this grand jury simulation. Include discussion about:
—What criteria did you use to determine whether someone should be charged with a crime?
—With what crimes did you consider charging which persons?
—Did you consider charging God with any crime? Why, or why not?
—What do you think about the judgments handed down by God upon the humans and the serpent at the end of Genesis 3?

(E) Note what God does.

- You will need newsprint, markerboard, or chalkboard and marker or chalk for this learning activity.
- The study book makes the case that God is the primary actor in Genesis 3. List on newsprint, markerboard, or chalkboard as participants call out the actions God takes in this chapter. One starting point is to look at the verbs used in those sentences in which God is the subject.
- Discuss:
—To what extent do you agree with the observation that God is the primary actor in Genesis 3?
—What exactly does God do in response to the first sin?
—To what extent does God follow through on God's statement in Genesis 2:16-17?

(F) Consider what the text teaches about God and about humanity.

- If your class members have not yet done so, take the time to have them read or review Genesis 3.
- Divide the class into groups of three. Instruct these small groups to pretend that all they have for a Bible is Genesis 3. Ask them to discuss: If all you had to go on was this passage, how would you describe God? How would you describe humanity?
- Ask small groups to share their descriptions with the whole class.

(G) Imagine the two trees.

- You will need art supplies such as drawing paper, markers, colored chalk, and crayons.
- Read or review the material presented in the sidebar, "The Two Trees," page 13 in the study book. Encourage persons to look up the biblical passages where the trees are mentioned in Genesis and elsewhere.

- Invite persons to imagine what they think the two trees might have looked like. Encourage them to consider abstract or symbolic images as well as literal ones. Some persons may wish to spend a few moments in quiet meditation focusing on the biblical texts and imagining what the trees might have looked like.
- Invite persons to use the provided art supplies to draw their depictions of the two trees.
- Provide time for persons to share what they drew and to discuss their experience of imagining the trees.
- Discuss: What relevance do these two trees have for us today?

Dimension 3: What Does the Bible Mean to Us?

(H) Think about what harm was done.

On the surface, eating a piece of fruit seems to be no big deal. We may be tempted to wonder what harm the first humans really did by eating that fruit. Similarly, sometimes today we hear some comments as "no harm, no foul" or that something is a "victimless crime." Moreover, some activities today are considered sins by some persons, usually on religious grounds, yet are not considered to be wrong by the general public. For example, although many religious groups and persons consider gambling to be sinful, most states in the United States today have legalized one or more forms of gambling.

- Discuss:
— Besides the punishments to which God sentenced the humans and the serpent, what harm did the first sin do to anyone?
— Why do you think God cared that the humans ate of the fruit of the tree of the knowledge of good and evil?
— What does consideration of this first sin tell us about the nature of sin for us today?
— What other examples can you think of in which some act is considered a sin but no one is apparently harmed by it? To what extent should it be considered a sin? Why?

(I) Hold a creative excuses contest.

- You will need newsprint and markers for each of the teams in this learning activity.
- If you have not already done so, draw attention to the ways that the first humans tried to avoid blame for their sin, as noted at the end of the section, "Taking Sin Seriously," pages 15–16 of the study book. Invite persons to read or review Genesis 3:8-13.
- Divide the class into teams of three or four persons.
- Assign each team this task: Pretend you are the first humans. You have just eaten the forbidden fruit. God has just confronted you. During the next five minutes, come up with as many excuses as you can to avoid being blamed for eating the fruit.
- When time is up, have the teams report on their excuses. Determine through applause, acclamation, or some other appropriate method the most creative excuse.
- Discuss:
— Did you find any of the excuses offered by the first humans in Genesis 3:8-13 to be plausible, persuasive, or at least worth considering?
— Would any excuse have been acceptable for avoiding blame under the circumstances of Genesis 2 and 3?
— In what ways do we try to avoid responsibility for our actions?
— In what ways do we accept responsibility for our actions?
— Are there any examples you are willing to share about times when you accepted responsibility for your actions? What were the results? What were your feelings?

(J) Debate the human condition after the Fall.

- Divide the class into two groups.
- Assign one group to come up with reasons why one might argue that "Life was better before the first humans 'bit the apple.'"
- Assign the other group to come up with reasons why one might argue that "Life became better after the first humans 'bit the apple.'"
- Let each group have three minutes to state their best arguments and two minutes to rebut the arguments of the other group.
- Allow time for persons to debrief both the experience of coming up with reasons for their side of the debate as well as the experience of the debate itself.
- Discuss:
— What difference does the reality of sin make in the way you live your life today?
— What difference does the description of God's response to the first sin make for the way you live your life today?

(K) Consider the power of shame.

- You will need newsprint or markerboard and markers or chalkboard and chalk.
- Read or summarize the material contained in the section, "The Power of Shame," page 17 in the study book.
- As an entire class or in smaller groups (depending upon the size of your class and the comfort participants have with one another), describe what shame feels like.

- One way to begin to describe what shame feels like is to list synonyms for shame. What other words mean the same or something similar to the word *shame*?
- Discuss:
—Do you agree with the perspective of the study book that "shame" and "vulnerability" are related?
—What examples can you offer in which feelings of shame, powerlessness, and fear are all mixed together?
—In what ways do you feel God is working today to ease shame and vulnerability in your life?

(L) Write a new ending.

- You will need to provide scratch paper and writing utensils for this learning activity.
- Ask class members individually to read Genesis 3. Instruct them as they read the passage this time to look specifically for those points where if one of the main characters—the serpent, the woman, the man, or God—had done something differently, the entire story would have ended differently. In other words, where are the dramatic turning points in this story?
- After reading the passage, ask class members individually to rewrite the story of the first sin in such a way that it ends differently. The one rule is that the ending must in some significant way be different from the one appearing in the biblical account.
- Divide the class into groups of three. Allow time for each person in these small groups to share their rewriting of the story. After each person has a chance to share, discuss—either in the small groups or in the class as a whole—these questions:
—What different "turning points" did you discover?
—What kinds of things did you imagine happening differently?
—In rewriting your story, did you think first about the turning point and then let events play themselves out naturally from that point? Or did you think about the ending you wanted to create and work backwards to an appropriate turning point? Or did you use some other method?
—In what ways do you think your changed story turned out better or worse than the story as told in the Bible?
—What lessons might be learned from your rewritten stories for living in today's world?

Additional Bible Helps

What About That Serpent?
The most mysterious and intriguing character ranging through the story of the first sin in Genesis 3 is easily the serpent. We have little actual information about the serpent available to us from the biblical text itself. If we rely only on Genesis 3 for our information, we can say no more than this about the serpent:
—he (a male pronoun is used in the New Revised Standard Version of the Bible to refer to the serpent) is a wild animal;
—he is a creature, created by God;
—he is crafty, meaning that he is intelligent in a shrewd, clever, and possibly devious way;
—he can talk(!);
—possibly, he moves in a manner different from the legless, slithering movement of modern snakes;
—for a motive or motives never made clear, he wants the first humans to transgress God's will;
—he is capable of deception;
—he is never given any opportunity to say anything in his defense; therefore, he makes no excuses nor gives any reasons for tempting the first humans into sin;
—he is apparently helpless in the face of God's judgment;
—he is never heard from again, at least not in the form he takes in the garden, and there is no direct evidence that he takes any other form.

As the sidebar, titled "The Power of Assumptions," on page 12 of the study book indicates, we sometimes read things into the Bible text that are not actually there. Nowhere in Genesis 3 itself is the serpent identified with Satan or the devil. Nowhere is the serpent explicitly characterized as evil or demonic. In fact, the serpent has very little character about him at all.

Bible scholar Walter Brueggemann has observed: "The serpent has been excessively interpreted. Whatever the serpent may have meant in earlier versions of the story, in the present narrative it has no independent significance. It is a technique to move the plot of the story. It is not a phallic symbol or satan or a principle of evil or death. It is a player in the dramatic presentation" (*Genesis: Interpretation: A Bible Commentary for Teaching and Preaching*, by Walter Brueggemann; John Knox Press, 1982; page 47).

Never again in the Old Testament is a serpent depicted in quite the same way. Serpents are generally viewed with distaste, though the reason may be nothing more than the cold-bloodedness of snakes and the possible belief of the time that all serpents were poisonous. The Hebrew word used for the serpent in Genesis 3 also is used for the "great sea monsters" created by God in Genesis 1:21, which have nothing whatsoever to do with the serpent of Genesis 3.

Only in the period between the writing of the Old and New Testaments does a figure known as Satan or the Devil begin to take shape within Jewish literature. In the few locations within the Old Testament itself where Satan—or "the satan"—is mentioned, it does not have a distinctive personality. Not until a couple of centuries before Christ does the figure of Satan take shape as an evil opponent of God. Previously, "the satan" who appears in Job 1 and 2 is a member of God's heavenly court who serves as something like a prosecuting attorney, is subordinate to God, and is neither necessarily antagonistic nor evil. In 1 Chronicles 21:1, a "satan" appears as possibly a spirit entering King David that incites him to inflict a census—considered as an oppressive event. However in the earlier written parallel passage of 2 Samuel 24:1, it is God who does the inciting out of wrath.

By the first century before Christ, Satan—which is the Hebrew word meaning the same as the Greek word *diabolos*, or "devil"—begins to be identified with the serpent of the garden. The Wisdom of Solomon—an "apocryphal" book appearing in the Greek version of the Old Testament considered authoritative by Eastern Orthodox and Roman Catholic Christians but not by Protestant Christians—offers one of the earliest examples of this identification: ". . . for God created us for incorruption, / and made us in the image of his own eternity, / but through the devil's envy death entered the world, / and those who belong to his company experience it" (Wisdom of Solomon 2:23-24).

By the time of the New Testament, the figure of Satan has solidified into an evil enemy of God and God's people. Perhaps the evil times upon which the people of Israel had fallen demanded a source in an equally evil opponent of Israel's God. In any case, the writer of the Book of Revelation sometime in the century after Christ explicitly identifies "that ancient serpent" with Satan, the Devil (Revelation 12:9-17).

Christians have inherited a tradition associating the serpent of the garden with Satan, the enemy of God. That tradition, however, cannot be traced back to the original text of Genesis 3.

3 Flood

Genesis 6:5-22
9:1-17

LEARNING MENU

Based on the learning needs of your class members, select at least one learning activity for each Dimension.

Dimension 1: What Does the Bible Say?

(A) Answer the Questions in Dimension 1.

Continue to encourage class members to work on answering the questions in the study book before they come to class. If necessary, you may wish to offer a brief time during the class session for individuals or teams to work on the questions.

- Invite class members to share and discuss their answers to the Dimension 1 questions in the study book. Help persons realize that many of the questions will not have only one, clear answer. Some questions may produce discussion as persons realize that the Bible text itself is ambiguous on a point or that different persons may have different understandings of particular texts.
- Responses to and discussions of the Dimension 1 questions may lead in these directions:

1. The quick answer to the question of how evil humanity was before the Flood is that it was *very* evil. Looking more closely at Genesis 6:5-13, we find that God considered humanity so incapable of doing anything except evil that God was sorry about ever creating humanity. Verses 11 and 13 imply that humanity's evil involved pervasive violence. Beyond that reference, we do not know what humanity's evil entailed.

2. Dimension 2 in the study book discusses Noah's righteousness. The Bible text itself does not specify anything in particular that Noah did that merited being saved from the Flood. However, the use of the term *righteousness* does imply that Noah's relationship with God was better than that held by the rest of humanity.

3. Genesis 8:20-21 states that as soon as Noah regained dry land, he built an altar and sacrificed burnt offerings to God of each species of ritually clean animals and birds. Verse 21 implies that Noah's sacrifice pleased God in such a way that God determined never again to destroy creation because of human wickedness.

4. The chart on page 14 compares what God did and said to Noah and his sons after the Flood with what God did and said to the first humans at Creation.

NOAH AND HIS SONS

"God blessed Noah and his sons, and said to them, 'Be fruitful and multiply, and fill the earth.'"
(Genesis 9:1)

"'The fear and dread of you shall rest on every animal of the earth, and on every bird of the air, on everything that creeps on the ground, and on all the fish of the sea; into your hand they are delivered. Every moving thing that lives shall be food for you; and just as I gave you the green plants, I give you everything. Only, you shall not eat flesh with its life, that is, its blood.'" (Genesis 9:2-4)

"Whoever sheds the blood of a human, by a human shall that person's blood be shed; for in his own image God made humankind."
(Genesis 9:6)

THE FIRST HUMANS

"God blessed them, and God said to them, 'Be fruitful and multiply, and fill the earth and subdue it.'"
(Genesis 1:28)

"See, I have given you every plant yielding seed that is upon the face of all the earth, and every tree with seed in its fruit; you shall have them for food." (Genesis 1:29)

"God created humankind in his image, in the image of God he created them; male and female he created them." (Genesis 1:27)

(B) Tell tales of starting over.

The story of the Flood is a story of starting over. God, disgusted by the wickedness, violence, and corruption of humanity, decides to destroy the world with water and start over again with a small remnant of survivors.

- Invite members of the class to tell stories of their own about starting over. Depending on the comfort level class members have with one another, these stories may be personal ones, or they may be ones from history or literature.
- If your class is large, you may want to split it into two or more groups for the telling of stories about starting over.

Dimension 2: What Does the Bible Mean?

(C) Consider the meaning of "righteousness."

- You will need to have on hand copies of reference resources such as Bible concordances, Bible dictionaries, standard dictionaries, and one-volume Bible commentaries. More than one copy of each type of reference resource will be helpful.
- Ask class members, individually or in small groups, to research the meaning of the word *righteousness*, in particular as it is used in reference to Noah. What does it mean for Noah to be called "righteous"?

You may find it helpful to do this research on your own ahead of class time. By doing so, you will gain experience in how to use the reference resources as well as add to your own knowledge about the meaning of *righteousness*. You will then be able to move around the room helping any persons who might need assistance in using the reference resources.

- Allow time for reports and discussion about the meaning of *righteousness* and about how the term applies to Noah.
- Discuss also:
—What does "righteousness" mean for us today?
—What does it look like to be "righteous" today?

(D) Make metaphors for the Flood.

- To set up the appropriate "climate" for this learning activity, you might want to pass around or post photographs of floods, such as those that appeared in *Time*, *Newsweek*, or *National Geographic* following the flooding of the Mississippi River basin in 1993.
- Divide the class members into teams of three or four persons, depending on how large your group is.
- Assign the teams the tasks of coming up with the greatest number *and* the most creative colloquial metaphors that relate in some way to the great Flood.
—To be most effective, metaphors should:
  1. have something to do with water or flooding;
  2. have something to do with the judgmental devastation involved in the Flood; and
  3. be in general circulation—that is, many persons are familiar with the saying or metaphor.

For example, one metaphor is the saying about something "going down the drain."
- As each team reports, let the entire class decide which metaphors should "count" toward a team's total, as well as decide which metaphor is the most creative. Applaud the winning team, as well as the efforts of all the teams.

(E) Pack to go on the ark.

Once the Flood began, the biblical text implies that the waters rose rapidly: "On that day all the fountains of the great deep burst forth, and the windows of the heavens were opened" (Genesis 7:11). "The waters swelled and increased greatly on the earth; and the ark floated on the face of the waters. The waters swelled so mightily on the earth that all the high mountains under the whole heaven were covered; the waters swelled above the mountains, covering them fifteen cubits deep" (Genesis 7:18-20).

One thing that the Flood meant was that there would be no going back once the rains began. Everything that Noah and his family had possessed or known before the Flood that had not been carried on the ark with them was utterly destroyed. They had to begin their new life after the Flood with only those things that they took on the ark with them.

- Divide the class members into small groups of two, three, or four persons. Assign them the task of coming up with a list of the items they think Noah and his family might have taken on the ark with them.
- If time permits, also ask the small groups to come up with a list of items they personally might take on an ark if they had advance warning of a coming great flood.
- One variation you might try if your class is made up of married couples is to ask husbands and wives to make up separate lists of items they would take on the ark without consulting with their spouse. Let spouses share lists and see how many items they had in common.

(F) Measure the ark.

- You will need measuring tapes and/or yardsticks. You will also need good weather and plenty of space outside.
- Allow time for persons to read or review the sidebar, "What's a Cubit?" page 22 of the study book.
- Take the class members outside. Using tape measures and yardsticks, ask class members to work together to measure off the approximate dimensions of the ark as given in Genesis 6:14-16. Or if your class members are adventurous as well as agile, let them try measuring off the dimensions of the ark using the traditional length of a cubit as determined by the distance from a person's elbow to his or her fingertips.
- Use your church building as a point of comparison for visualizing the size of the ark according to the Bible.
- Allow time for persons to share what they imagine it might be like to stay in a vessel the size of the ark for over ten months. Remember, you would also have all those animals on board!

Dimension 3:
What Does the Bible Mean to Us?

(G) Try to listen for God.

- Summarize the material from "Righteousness in a Wicked World," pages 24–25 in the study book; or ask the class to read or review it.
- Discuss the statement from the study book: "The key to understanding Noah may be contained in the sentence, 'Noah walked with God' (Genesis 6:9). Noah, among all the human beings of his generation, was the one person who took God seriously. He was the lone person who had prepared his heart to listen in the presence of God when God said, 'Make yourself an ark. . . .'"
—To what extent do you agree or disagree with the statement?
—How do you understand the Bible's comment that "Noah walked with God"?
—How do you individually seek to "walk with God"? How do you individually try to take God seriously?
—How do you collectively as a class seek to "walk with God"? How do you as a class try to take God seriously?
—How does your congregation seek to "walk with God"? How does your congregation try to take God seriously?
—What might you individually, as a class, or as a congregation do to take God more seriously?
- If you have time, teach your class this way of preparing their hearts to listen to God better:
—Ask persons to sit comfortably in their seats, preferably with both feet flat on the floor and resting both hands gently on their laps.
—Instruct them to close their eyes and to breathe normally. Tell them to spend a few moments concentrating on the air moving in and out of their bodies. "Let your focus become your breathing. If you hear other noises, just hear them and then let them roll over you. If thoughts come to mind, let them flow into and out of your consciousness. As you do so, just try to be in silence."
—Allow a good two or three minutes in silence.
—Instruct persons to say the following prayer silently in rhythm with their breathing over and over: "Gracious Lord / God of Noah / help me better / to walk with you."
—Allow at least another two or three minutes for persons to practice breathing that prayer.
—Tell persons that as they become ready, they should gently open their eyes and return to focusing on the class.

- Allow anyone who wishes to share about their experience to do so.

  Note that this type of prayer is sometimes called a "breath prayer" (so called because one prays in rhythm with one's breathing) and that one can pray in this way with any appropriate words in rhythm with one's breathing anytime and anywhere.

(H) Act less violently.

Summarize or review the material from "Reducing Violence" on pages 25–26 of the study book.
- Discuss the questions posed at the end of that section:
—What awareness do you have of violence in your world today? (If you need a way to get discussion started, you might have small groups browse through a week or two's worth of newspapers in order to clip or note headlines and articles relating to violence.)
—In what ways does violence touch you personally?
—In what ways do you participate in violence?
—In what specific ways can you and the members of your class do one specific thing that might reduce the violence present in your world?
- Challenge class members to agree to undertake and to support one another in doing one specific thing that might reduce the violence present in the world.

(I) Ponder starting over.

Note the statement on page 25 of the study book: "The Flood itself was not an act of dreadful punishment directed against the mass of humanity. Rather, the Flood stemmed from God's desire to 'wash' the world clean, to start all over with creation from scratch. . . . God was not concerned with the fate of the wicked human beings so much as God wanted to start over with a new creation."
- Discuss the extent to which class members agree with the statement.
- Divide the class into small groups. Ask small groups to imagine that they are the human remnant who have survived a modern catastrophe on the order of the great Flood. What would they do in the minutes, days, weeks, and years after stepping off of the new ark? What, if anything, would they do differently from what they do now?

Additional Bible Helps

Where Did the Ark Land?
Despite volumes of books and hours of television programs, we cannot today say with any certainty where precisely Noah's ark landed. Nor is it likely that the remains of the actual ark described in the Bible will ever be found, photographed, or excavated. *It would be extremely unusual for a cypress-wood-and-pitch vessel to survive millennia in a recognizable form.*

As the study book indicates, the biblical text itself makes no reference to the ark landing at "Mount Ararat." The New Revised Standard Version of the Bible only refers to "the mountains of Ararat." Later Jewish, Christian, and Muslim traditions, however, sought to identify particular mountains as the actual site the ark made landfall.

The "Curse" of Ham
One of the most regrettable chapters in the history of biblical understanding centers upon the story of the so-called curse of Noah's son, Ham, as told in Genesis 9:18-27.

After the Flood, Noah becomes the world's first vine-dresser and vintner. He also apparently becomes the world's first drunk. Genesis 9:21 states that Noah "drank some of the wine and became drunk, and he lay uncovered in his tent." Specifically, this verse means that Noah passed out either stark naked or sprawled in such a manner that he lay with his genitals exposed.

Verse 22 indicates that in some manner that the first readers of Genesis would have understood, Ham—one of Noah's sons—shows disrespect for his father and his father's sexuality. That was a grievous offense within that culture and time! Though Ham tells his brothers Shem and Japheth about what he saw, Shem and Japheth show appropriate respect by averting their eyes from Noah's nakedness and covering him with a blanket. Upon sobering up, Noah punishes his youngest son with a curse. But note who Noah curses in verses 25-27! And hold that note for a moment.

The curse has been understood to condemn Ham to slavery at the hands of his brothers. Earlier generations read this curse as applying to Ham's descendants, including his son Cush and *his* descendants in turn. Because the inhabitants of the land of Cush in Africa were black-skinned, some persons read into this curse a religious justification for the enslavement of black persons of African heritage.

Today we would abhor such an interpretation of this biblical text. Besides being a perversion of biblical and Christian ethics, such a reading is also a perversion of the Bible's words themselves. Noah's pronouncement of the curse is peculiar because as you have already noted, Noah curses not *Ham* but Ham's son *Canaan*—the brother of Cush and the ancestor of the Canaanites whom the Israelites centuries later displace from the land of Canaan.

Rather than a biblical justification for the enslavement of black-skinned persons of African heritage, this curse really serves as one explanation for the conquest of the Canaanites and their expulsion from the land that Israel then came to occupy. If there be any religious justification for enslavement in this passage, it is a justification for the enslavement of the Canaanites of Old Testament times because of their sexual practices considered by Israelites as immoral.

One Christian Interpretation of the Great Flood

If we view the story of the great Flood from God's perspective, it is mostly a story of judgment and disgust in the face of human wickedness and a story of starting creation over from scratch. If we view the story from humanity's point of view, it becomes a story of survival. By God's great graciousness, a few human beings survived the Flood. By God's action they were saved from drowning with the rest of humanity. In this sense, the story of the great Flood is a story about salvation.

First Peter 3:18-22 is a difficult, strange passage, especially verse 19 that apparently speaks of Christ preaching to the spirits of those who had died during Noah's time. Set that portion of the text aside for this time. Instead focus on how First Peter interprets the Flood as a symbol for baptism. The waters that the Flood and that baptism share in common are seen as a symbol of salvation. Noah and his companions on the ark were *saved* by the waters of the Flood. Indeed the waters that drowned the rest of humanity *lifted* the inhabitants of the ark to safety and brought them to a new, clean world.

Similarly the text of the third chapter of First Peter points to the saving waters of baptism "not as a removal of dirt from the body, but as an appeal to God for a good conscience, through the resurrection of Jesus Christ." The great Flood foreshadows Christian baptism as a vehicle of salvation and new life.

4

Genesis 11:1-9

Pride and Confusion

LEARNING MENU
Based on what you know about your class members, their needs, and the ways in which they learn best, choose at least one learning activity from each of the Dimensions.

Dimension 1: What Does the Bible Say?

(A) Take a tall field trip.

- Identify the tallest point accessible to you and members of your class within your church building (or the building in which you meet). If any of your class members have difficulty walking or climbing stairs, identify the tallest point to which everyone can gain easy access. Preferably, find a place in or near that tallest point from which persons can safely see outside or some point inside that is some distance below.
- For example, a church building might provide easy and safe access to a window or observation point high up in a steeple. Or another church building might offer a balcony overlooking the sanctuary. If your church building only has one story, you might have to become creative to provide a field trip to a "tall" point, or simply bypass this learning activity. Whatever tall point you choose to lead your class to, be sure that everyone in the class can readily reach that place.
- When your class members have gathered, lead them to the tall point you have identified. You may wish to leave a note so that latecomers know where to find you and the rest of their class.
- When you reach the tall point, ask the class members to look around, especially observing what they can from any window or observation point that permits them to look below.
- If there is room for class members at least to stand comfortably at the tall point, hold the following discussion there. If there is not room, or if some persons cannot comfortably stand, then return to your normal meeting room to hold your discussion.
- Discuss:
—What did you see from the vantage point of the tall point to which we went?
—What did you feel as you climbed up to the tall point? What did you feel as you looked out from that place?
—What did you fear as you climbed up to the tall point? What did you fear as you looked out from that place?
—What memories, significance, or experiences do other tall places hold for you?
- Read aloud the story of the Tower of Babel to the class (Genesis 11:1-9). Ask: What connections can you make between your experiences on your field trip to a tall

place, or from your remembered experiences of other tall places, and the story of the Tower of Babel?

(B) Discuss the Dimension 1 questions.

- We cannot stress strongly enough that the best approach to dealing with Dimension 1 questions is to ask class members to read the Bible passage and to answer the Dimension 1 questions *before* they come to class. Your limited class time will be best spent in supplementing the reading and work your class members have already done.
- However, if many of your class members have not worked on their Dimension 1 questions before class, you may want to provide them with a brief amount of class time to read the Bible passage and to answer their questions. Asking class members to work on their answers in groups of two or three can provide an opportunity for persons to learn from each other and to develop relationships.
- Class discussion of Dimension 1 questions may take these directions:
  1. Genesis 11:3-4 offers at least three possible motives for the building of the tower. Verse 4 suggests that the humans might have desired to reach the heavens. Perhaps the humans wanted to reach the heavens in order to gain better access to God; that is, they wanted to communicate better with God. Or another reason for reaching the heavens might have been that the humans sought to rival God and possibly to usurp God's place as God. Verse 4 also suggests a third motive: the humans wanted to make a name for themselves. They either wanted to make sure that their fame endured forever or they wanted to make sure that they were not forgotten.
  2. Verse 5 offers a little irony: The great tower is so puny from God's point of view that God has to leave heaven and come down in order to see the human city and tower. From this perspective, the humans failed in their goal. However, verse 6 implies that the humans did well enough in their goal to gain God's attention and cause God to decide that the humans had best be scattered and confused to prevent future grand projects.
  3. Nowhere does the biblical text say that God considered what the humans were doing to be a threat to God. Verse 6 implies that God was concerned lest the humans go on to possibly more harmful projects in their arrogance if they succeeded in building their tower and city.
  4. The result of the building project was their scattering across the face of the earth and the confusion of their languages (of their unity and communication efforts). Yet one might make the case that they succeeded in their goal of "making a name" for themselves in a backhanded sort of way. Certainly the would-be builders of the Tower of Babel remain famous today, though not for the reasons they had intended.

Dimension 2: What Does the Bible Mean?

(C) Build your own tower.

- You will need an adequate supply of Tinker Toy® building toys, blocks, or building materials such as modeling clay and toothpicks.
- Divide the class members into two or more teams. Challenge the teams to see which team can build the tallest free-standing tower from their building materials in five minutes. Only the supplied building materials may be used in their towers. They must build their towers on top of the table (or other suitable surface you decide upon in advance so that all towers start from the same level). Their towers must be able to stand by themselves without support.
- After the five minutes are up, declare a winner. Then discuss these questions.
—What did you learn about tower building?
—In what ways did your team feel and express the desire to build the tallest tower? Why did your team want to build the tallest tower?
—How did it feel to win (or lose) the contest to build the tallest tower?
—What did your efforts teach you about the significance of unity and communication in human projects?
—What did your own tower building experience teach you that relates to the Bible story of the building of the Tower of Babel?

(D) Debate the building of the Tower of Babel.

- Provide copies of Bible dictionaries, concordances, and one-volume commentaries.
- Divide the class members into two teams.
- Assign one team the task of developing arguments in support of saying that the people of Babel were *right* to build their tower. Assign the other team the task of developing arguments in support of saying that the people of Babel were *wrong* to build their tower. Make sure each team selects a spokesperson.
- Allow time for teams to read or review Genesis 11:1-9, to research their side of the argument in the Bible reference books you have supplied, and to work together on building their arguments.
- After ten or fifteen minutes to complete their work, ask

team spokespersons to report on the arguments their teams developed.
- Ask class members to leave behind their team identity and to discuss which set of arguments seems more persuasive to them.

(E) Discuss making "names" for yourselves.

- Review Genesis 11:4, noting how one motivation for the humans to build their city and tower was their urgent desire to "make a name" for themselves. Note also that they apparently wanted to make sure that the world (and the heavens?) noticed their mighty works because of insecurity. They were fearful that if they were not famous for their great deeds, they would be overwhelmed by other forces and "scattered abroad upon the face of the whole earth."
- Discuss:
—In the light of Genesis 11:1-9, what appears to be wrong with "making a name" for oneself?
—Are there any good reasons in favor of "making a name" for oneself? If so, what might those be?
—How do we go about trying to make names for ourselves in our time? What kind of efforts do we make as individuals? What kind of efforts do we make in the name of a group, a nation, or humanity as a whole?
—What are our motivations for trying to make names for ourselves? To what extent are these efforts appropriate? To what extent do they fall under the same judgment as the Tower of Babel?
—To what extent are we successful in our modern attempts to make names for ourselves? To what extent do we find ourselves thwarted? What are the results of being successful or finding ourselves thwarted at trying to make names for ourselves?

Dimension 3: What Does the Bible Mean to Us?

(F) Consider God's vision for humanity today.

- Read or review the section entitled, "Whose Vision?" on page 32 of the study book.
- Divide the class members into groups of three or four.
- Ask the groups first to review Chapters 1 and 2 of Genesis, noting the expressions of God's will for humanity found there. They may also wish to review the material in Chapter 1 of the study book.
- Ask the groups to discuss:
—How would you describe God's vision for humanity as expressed in Chapters 1 and 2 of Genesis?
—How well have modern humans fulfilled or worked toward God's vision for them?
—In what ways might God have (or not have) a different vision for humanity now than the vision expressed in Chapters 1 and 2 of Genesis?
- Allow time for groups to share and discuss their finding with the whole class.

(G) Consider your congregation's vision.

- Ask the class members to read or review the section entitled, "Whose Vision?" on page 32 of the study book.
- Divide the class members into groups of three or four persons.
- Ask the groups to work on describing what their congregation's vision is. A vision might be defined as a statement consistent with a person's or group's reason for being that pulls them into the future by providing a glimpse of what that future is desired to be. For example, God's vision for creation as expressed in Chapters 1 and 2 of Genesis involved a future in which humanity had been fruitful, had multiplied, and had filled the earth.
- Discuss within groups:
—How do you know what the vision of your congregation is?
—If your congregation has a formal statement of its vision, by what methods was it developed? In what ways are those methods adequate or inadequate to the task of arriving at an understanding of the congregation's vision?
—To what extent do you think that your congregation's vision is consistent with God's vision for it?
—What movement do you see by and within your congregation toward fulfilling the vision you have described for it? What do members of your congregation need to do to move it further toward fulfilling that vision?
- Allow time for the groups to share and discuss their findings with the entire class.

(H) Seek God's vision for you and your class.

- Ask the class members to read or review the material in the section entitled, "Whose Vision?" on page 32 in the study book.
- Invite class members to participate in a guided meditation experience based on the Tower of Babel story in Genesis 11:1-9. A guided meditation experience seeks prayerfully to ask God for discernment of God's truth. Often, as in this case, a guided meditation focuses and reflects upon a particular Bible text. One of the keys to guided meditation is for participants to seek to move

beyond their own assumptions and to truly open themselves up to listening for what God might say to them.
- Ask participants to sit comfortably, preferably with both feet resting flat on the floor and hands resting gently on their laps. Ask them to close their eyes and to become aware of their breathing. Focusing momentarily on their breathing in and out will help chase away outside distractions.
- Announce that you will read aloud the Bible passage found in Genesis 11:1-9. Ask persons to listen to your reading and to imagine themselves as one of the people on the plain of Shinar [SHIGH-nahr]. Proceed to read Genesis 11:1-9 in a slow, gentle voice.
- Pause after you finish the reading. Allow one or two minutes for persons to continue to reflect upon the passage in silence. Then announce that you will read the same passage a second time. This time persons should listen to your reading while imagining themselves as standing at the side of God. Proceed to read Genesis 11:1-9 in a slow, gentle voice.
- Again pause after you finish the reading. Allow one or two minutes for persons to continue to reflect upon the passage in silence. Then announce that you will read the same passage one last time. This time persons should listen to your reading while permitting their imagination to take them wherever it will. Encourage them to explore whatever aspects of the passage to which their imagination takes them because sometimes that is God's Spirit leading them to look at something important. Read Genesis 11:1-9 in a slow, gentle voice.
- Pause again, allowing one or two minutes for persons to reflect upon the passage in silence. Then ask them to open their eyes and prepare to share together in class.
- Discuss:
—What did you experience during the guided meditation?
—What new, possibly significant insights did you encounter?
—What sense did you have of God's Spirit leading or nudging you during this experience?
—What did this guided meditation help you to see about God's vision?
—What do you think or feel about this kind of guided meditation experience? How might you use it in your personal Bible study?

(I) Identify modern towers of Babel.

- Ask the class members to read or review "Towers and Technology," pages 33–34 in the study book.
  The study book suggests that modern efforts to explore space, to explore the possibilities of nuclear power, and to discover the secrets of human genetic makeup bear some resemblances to the efforts of the ancient humans of the plain of Shinar to build their tower. Discuss as a class the extent to which members agree with this observation.
- Divide the class members into groups of three or four. Assign the small groups the task of agreeing upon one modern human endeavor that they believe most closely resembles the effort to build the Tower of Babel. They may choose one of the efforts mentioned in the study book or come up with a different one of their own.
- Allow time for groups to report and discuss their findings.

TOWER OF BABEL (GENESIS 11:1-9)

| "So the LORD scattered them abroad from there over the face of all the earth." (Genesis 11:8) | "Come, let us build ourselves . . . a tower with its top in the *heavens*." (Genesis 11:4) | "Come, let us go down, and confuse their language there, so that they will not understand one another's speech." (Genesis 11:7) | ". . . this is only the beginning of what [the humans] will do; nothing that they propose to do will now be impossible for them." (Genesis 11:6) | ". . . let us make a *name* for ourselves. . . ." (Genesis 11:4) |

FIRST CHRISTIAN PENTECOST (ACTS 2:1-47)

| "When the day of Pentecost had come, they were all together in one place." (Acts 2:1) | "And suddenly from *heaven* there came a sound like the rush of a violent wind. . . ." (Acts 2:2) | "And at this sound the crowd gathered and was bewildered, because each one heard them speaking in the native language of each." (Acts 2:6) | ". . . in our own languages we hear them speaking about God's deeds of power." (Acts 2:11) | "Repent, and be baptized every one of you in the *name* of Jesus Christ so that your sins may be forgiven." (Acts 2:38) |

Additional Bible Helps

The Curse of Babel Reversed
Flip ahead pages and millennia in your Bible to read Acts 2:1-47, the story of the first Christian Pentecost.

Christian Bible scholars, theologians, and preachers have long noted how Luke appears intentionally to frame his telling of the first Christian Pentecost in terms that suggest the removal or the reversal of the curse of Babel as the Holy Spirit came upon the disciples gathered in Jerusalem. The chart on page 21 contrasts the Tower of Babel story in Genesis 11 and the first Christian Pentecost story in Acts 2.

The Plain of Shinar
The region called the plain of Shinar in Genesis 11 was a truly important area before, during, and after Old Testament times. If you are interested in a more detailed look at the history of this region, you might use a Bible dictionary to look up the place names, *Shinar*, *Mesopotamia*, *Sumer*, *Assyria*, and *Babylon*. These names were applied in ancient times to refer to the fertile region between the Tigris and Euphrates rivers and that region's peoples. The empires that rose under the names *Assyria* and *Babylon* in particular play a large part in the later history of the people of Israel. In fact we shall soon learn in this study that Abraham and Sarah, the foreparents of the people of Israel, will first come from this region between the rivers.

The Ancient Near East Before Abraham

The Babylonian Empire

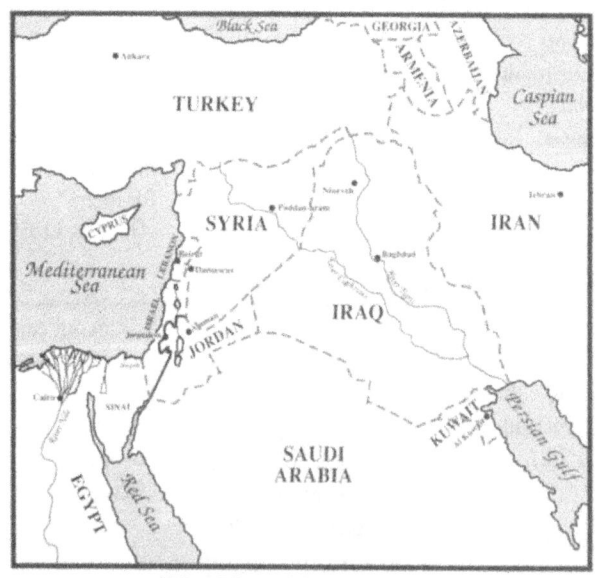

The Near East Today

Covenant and Sojourn

Genesis 12:1-9; 15:1-21

LEARNING MENU
Based on what you know about your class members, their needs, and the ways in which they learn best, choose at least one learning activity from each of the Dimensions.

Dimension 1: What Does the Bible Say?

(A) Study Abram's map.

No, Abram probably did not have a map of the region into which he moved from Ur and Haran. If he did, that map certainly has not survived into our time. However, many persons will benefit from a study of a map drawn today of the region through which Abram and Sarai passed on their sojourn. Reasons for doing a map study include learning what the geographical settings of Abram and Sarai were like; understanding the significance of their traveling through various cities and areas; and becoming familiar with locations, pronunciations, and modern equivalents of important places mentioned in the Bible.

Keep in mind as you undertake this map study that some members of your class may have difficulty reading a map. This does not mean they are less intelligent than persons who excel at map reading. Map reading involves some aptitudes that not everyone possesses. Different adults will have differing abilities.

- You might want to have available one or more large, modern maps of the region discussed in this chapter. Today, that region would include the modern nations of Kuwait, Iraq, Turkey, Syria, Lebanon, Jordan, Egypt, and Israel, including the parts of Israel placed under Palestinian self-rule in 1994. One good source of such maps are recent copies of *National Geographic*. Be careful that any modern map you share with the class has not been made obsolete by political changes. As they work on their map study, encourage class members to compare where biblical locations would show up on these modern maps.

- Divide the class into groups of two or three. Ask groups to turn to the map on page 36 of the study book. Group members should then work together to read Genesis 12:1-9 and 15:1-21 through verse-by-verse. As they read, groups should pause to note any place names appearing in these passages. They should take the time to identify places on the map and to look up references to those places in the sidebar "The Times and Places of Abram and Sarai," pages 38–39 of the study book.

- You might want to have one or more Bible atlases on hand for use by those class members who are intrigued by map study and want to learn more using maps showing greater detail than the one in the study book.

- You might also want persons to share within their

groups their responses to questions 3 and 4 in Dimension 1 on page 37 of the study book. These questions ask persons to mark on their study book maps.

(B) Answer Dimension 1 questions.

- Continue to encourage class members to read the Bible material and to work on the Dimension 1 questions before the class session. By doing so, everyone will learn more quickly about the Bible passage under discussion. You will want, however, to mix patience with your gentle persistence. Today's adults—especially those of the so-called "boomer" generation and younger (roughly age fifty and younger) are less likely to undertake class preparation or "homework" than were their elders at the same age.
- If many of your class members have not worked on their Dimension 1 questions, provide a limited amount of time for them to read the Bible passage and to work on the four Dimension 1 questions. Two of those questions involve using the map on page 36 of the study book.

- Directions that discussions of these questions might take are:
  1. The LORD makes these promises to Abram in Genesis 12:1-9:
     —"I will make of you a great nation";
     —"I will bless you";
     —"I will make your name great";
     —"I will bless those who bless you, and the one who curses you I will curse";
     —"in you all the families of the earth shall be blessed";
     —"To your offspring I will give this land" (referring to Canaan).
     The LORD makes these promises to Abram in Genesis 15:1-21:
     —"I am your shield";
     —"your reward shall be very great";
     —"no one but your very issue shall be your heir";
     —Abram's descendants shall be as countless as the stars in the heavens;
     —"To your descendants I give this land";
     —Some Bible scholars believe that verses 13-16

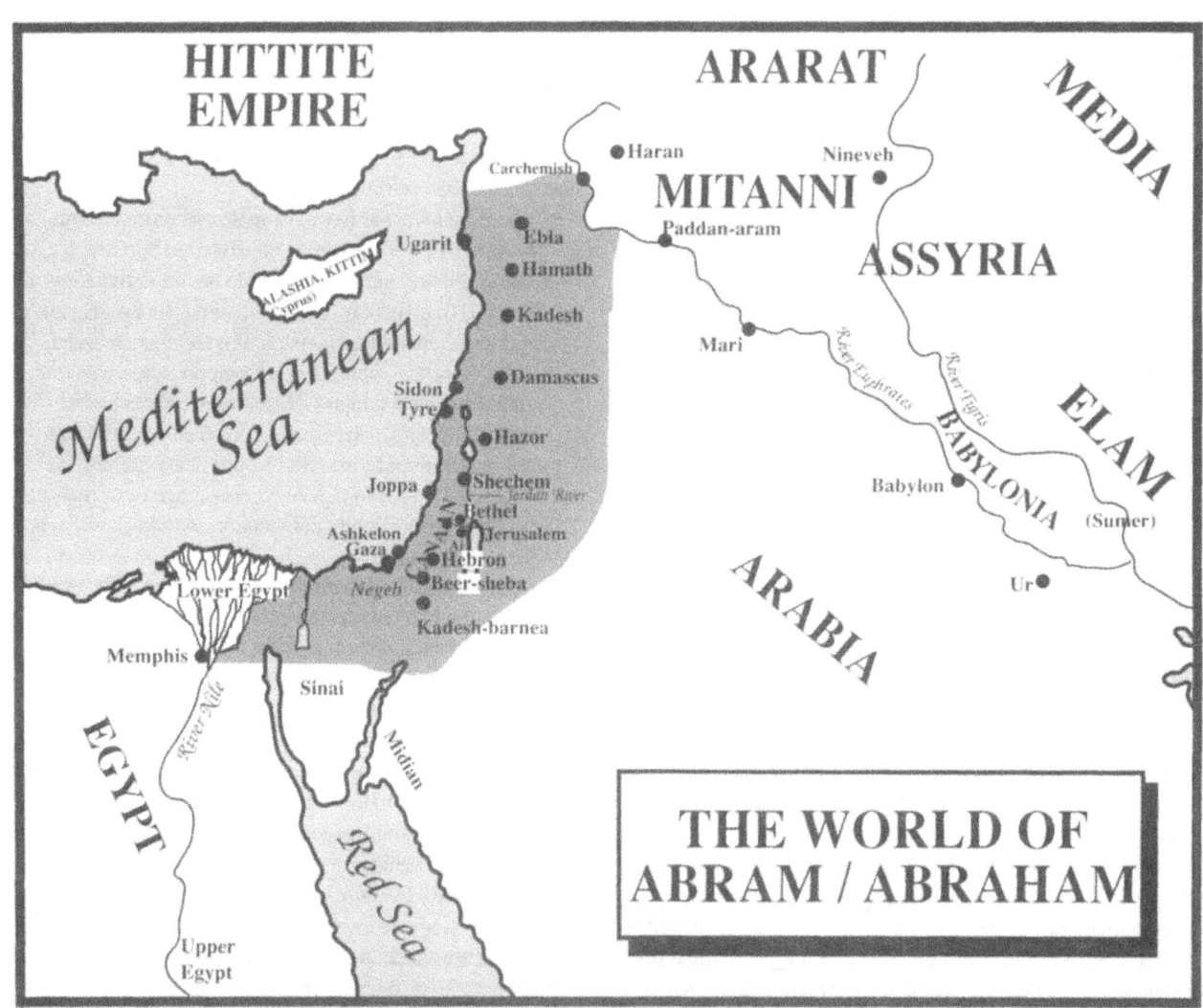

24

JOURNEY THROUGH THE BIBLE

were inserted at a later time in order to explain the delay in the fulfillment of God's promise of land until after the Exodus from slavery in Egypt.

2. The two promises that are the most similar between these two passages are the promises to give Abram many descendants ("make of you a great nation") and to give to Abram's descendants the land of Canaan.

3. There is no way of knowing for sure the exact route taken by Abram, Sarai, and their people from Haran to the Negeb. Established routes, terrain, the need to find adequate food and water for both humans and livestock, and detours caused by necessities and distractions of various sorts would mean that their route was probably not a straight line between the points in Genesis 12:4-9. And yet the best we can probably do is to draw lines between those points:
   —Haran;
   —Shechem;
   —the hill country between Bethel on the west and Ai on the east;
   —the Negeb.

   Encourage class members to look up information about these locations in the sidebar entitled, "The Times and Places of Abram and Sarai," on pages 38–39 of the study book.

4. The shaded area should cover the land between the Euphrates River in Mesopotamia (modern Iraq) to the Nile River in Egypt. This territory roughly describes the extent of King David's kingdom during the early part of the tenth century before Christ.

Dimension 2: What Does the Bible Mean?

(C) Discover the meaning of names.

- You will need to provide copies of Bible dictionaries. If you have them available, several different versions of Bible dictionaries would be helpful.
- Point out that although we may feel familiar with the names *Abraham* and *Sarah*, when we first meet them in the Bible they are named *Abram* and *Sarai*.
- Divide the class members into two groups. If you have a very large class, you may want to divide them into an even number of small groups of three to seven persons each. In this case, assign half the groups to each of the two tasks.
- Assign one group (or half of the groups) the task of looking up the names *Abram* and *Abraham* in one or more Bible dictionaries. From what they learn and already know about Abraham, ask them to speculate on why his name might have been changed by God from Abram to Abraham.
- Assign the other group (or half of the groups) the task of looking up the names *Sarai* and *Sarah* in one or more Bible dictionaries. From what they learn and already know about Sarah, ask them to speculate on why her name might have been changed by God from Sarai to Sarah.
- Allow time for groups to report and discuss their findings and speculations.

(D) Visit the places Abram and Sarai visited.

- You will need a variety of Bible atlases, Bible commentaries, concordances, and Bible dictionaries. If you have limited resources, at least try to provide one of each.
- Divide the class members into small groups. Assign groups at least one of the following places visited by Abram and Sarai according to Genesis 12:1-9:
   —Haran
   —Canaan
   —Shechem
   —Bethel
   —Ai
   —the Negeb
- Ask groups to research their assigned places using their Bibles and the reference tools you have provided. If your church has a library, groups may wish to do their research there.
- Ask the groups to discover at least the following in the course of their research:
   —Where is this place located?
   —What other points of interest is it near?
   —In what modern country would it be located today?
   —Is there a modern city or region on the same site?
   —What might that place have been like in the time of Abram and Sarai?
   —Is there any indication of the population and the ethnic makeup of the inhabitants at the time of Abram and Sarai?
   —What kind of terrain did that place have?
   —What else happened at that place within biblical history?

(E) Update Abram and Sarai.

- Divide the class members into groups of three to five persons each.
   Note that sometimes in order to understand some things about biblical personages, persons may find it helpful to use their imaginations and to think of those biblical persons in terms of what they would be like today.
- Make sure that groups take time to read Genesis 12:1-9 and 15:1-21 if they have not already done so.

- Ask groups to play around with imagining what these passages about Abram and Sarai would be like if they took place today. Emphasize that this is intended to be a *playful* activity.
- Among the areas that groups might discuss include:
—What today would be as much of a break with the comfortable past as Abram and Sarai leaving Haran?
—What today would mean such a degree of hopelessness as the infertility of Abram and Sarai did in their time?
—What promises might God make to a modern-day Abram and Sarai that would be as meaningful today as the promises to Abram were in his time?
- Ask groups to share and discuss their findings with the whole class.

(F) Research the concept of covenant.

The concept of *covenant* is one of the most important concepts in the Bible. This theme is found throughout the entire Bible. In fact, the term *testament*, as in Old Testament and New Testament, means "covenant." Therefore it is very important that persons understand what the Bible means in the concept of *covenant* if they are to understand what they read in the Bible.

- You will need to provide copies of Bible dictionaries, concordances, and one-volume commentaries. A variety of each type of Bible reference tool will be helpful if you have access to them.
- In groups of three to five persons, ask class members to research the concept of *covenant*. They should use the Bible reference tools that you have provided for them. The sidebar, "What Is a Covenant?" is one starting point (page 40 in the study book).
- Ask groups to share and discuss their findings with the entire class. Be sure to point out how different groups may have learned different things about *covenant*, helping the entire class fill out its understanding.
- Because this is such a major theme in the Bible, you may want to allow a significant amount of time for this learning activity, depending on what else you want to accomplish with this session.
- One alternative to in-class research might be to ask individuals or teams to research the concept of covenant on their own either during the week before this session or over one or two weeks following. If you take this alternative, be sure to plan for in-class time for persons to share and discuss their findings.
- One set of key questions your class can discuss to help them wrap up a discussion on covenant and move into looking at what the Bible means for them is
—What covenant does God have with what persons today?
—How do you know about that covenant?
—Is that covenant being kept?

Dimension 3: What Does the Bible Mean to Us?

(G) Study one New Testament commentary on Abram.

- You will need to have one-volume Bible commentaries and/or commentaries on the Letter to the Hebrews.
- Summarize or review the material in "Humanity as God Intended," page 41 in the study book.
   Note that at least two passages in Hebrews serve as a commentary on Abraham's faith and righteousness:
   —Hebrews 6:13-20
   —Hebrews 11:1-19
- Ask your class, individually or in teams, to study how those two passages interpret the material found in Genesis 12:1-9 and 15:1-21.
- Among the questions persons may want to consider are
—In what ways do the Hebrews passages seem to draw directly upon passages from Genesis?
—In the course of your research did you find other passages in Hebrews that appear to comment on these Genesis passages concerning Abraham?
—In what ways is the commentary on Abraham found in Romans 4 similar to and/or different from that found in Hebrews?
—What information can you find about the writing of the Letter to the Hebrews and its first audience that gives you any insight into its commentary on Abraham? (Many Bibles include a brief article covering the background of a book of the Bible immediately preceding that book.)

(H) Anticipate your future.

We might say that one of the main themes in the story of Abram and Sarai is that of *anticipating the future*. Before God's movement into their lives, Abram and Sarai can see no future before them because they are childless in their old age. Only in God's promises to them are they able to anticipate any sort of future.

- Review with the class members the themes in the above paragraph. Then ask them to spend three minutes (as you time it on a clock) contemplating their own futures.
- After the three minutes, ask class members to share as they wish about their contemplations of the future.
- Next ask them to spend another three minutes contemplating what effect God has upon their future.
- Discuss:
—How do you anticipate that your future will be different because of God?
—What kind of response will you have to make to God in order for God to have an effect on your future?

—How do you anticipate that the future of your congregation could be different because of God?

Additional Bible Helps

A Covenant Ritual

In Genesis 15:7-12, 17-18, God and Abram seal their covenant with a ritual. Many scholars believe that this segment of the text comes from a very early tradition. Modern persons have nothing contemporary with which to compare this ritual. To our senses, the ritual strikes us as bizarre and fearsome, yet somehow coming from the shadow side of reality. There is a sense of the truly awesome, awful aspect of God in this passage. We have a sensation of being in the presence of the other-worldly.

In verse 7, God states unequivocally who God is, what God has done, and what God will do. It is a majestic statement. Incredibly, Abram challenges God. Abram does not dispute God's identity. Nor does he deny that he came to Canaan in response to God's call. But Abram wants a guarantee that God will do what God has promised. So God offers to go through a ritual as a guarantee.

God commands Abram to bring five animals: a heifer, a female goat, a ram, a turtledove, and a pigeon. These are all animals commonly offered as sacrifices. The people of Israel will later consider all of them to be among ritually clean animals.

The animals, but not the birds, are cut in half, with the halves laid opposite each other, in two parallel rows. Verse 11 adds "color" to the narrative. We can easily visualize Abram, anxious to gain a guarantee from God about this too-wonderful promise, shooing the hungry vultures away from feasting on *his* ritual animals.

Verse 12 is the stuff that raises goose bumps on the flesh of arms and legs, that stirs the hairs on backs of necks: "As the sun was going down, a deep sleep fell upon Abram, and a deep and terrifying darkness descended upon him." Within the context of this "deep sleep" Abram receives God's word to him: "Know this for certain. . . ."

We cannot hope to figure out the "deep sleep." Was it a dream? Was it a trance? Was it some other altered state of consciousness? Is it something that we might hope (or dare to desire) to duplicate within our own experience? Whatever the reality of this twilight encounter, the presence of God—which previously had been comfortable to Abram (remember how Abram had dared to challenge God to prove that the promise would be kept?)—is now *terrifying*.

In whatever state of consciousness Abram enjoys at the fall of night, he sees "a smoking fire pot and a flaming torch" passing between the halves of the animal carcasses. God appears as fire to Abram, just as centuries later God will appear to Moses as a burning bush. We need carefully to keep in mind that the fire is not God, nor is God in the fire. Instead, either God's presence is symbolized or represented by fire, or God's appearance on this occasion is best likened to fire. In this latter case, we need to acknowledge that human language cannot adequately describe the completeness of either the reality or the appearance of God.

The key action in this passage is God—visualized as two types of fire—moving between the halves of the carcasses Abram had prepared. Many scholars believe that when humans of that time engaged in the same kind of ritual, the person passing between the carcass halves was saying, in effect, "Let the same dismemberment happen to me if I fail to keep my promise!"

If this is an accurate understanding of this ritual, then God is saying to Abram, "I—the LORD God—will undergo dismemberment if I fail to keep my promise to give you this land!"

Abram has his guarantee. He challenged God's ability or willingness to keep the promise of land, and God responded. There are two ways to take God's guarantee to Abram, both of which are startling. One possible interpretation is that God will actually become vulnerable to being torn asunder should God fail to keep this promise. The other interpretation is that God is saying there is as much chance of God becoming split apart like those carcasses as there is of God failing to keep the promise that is so crucial to Abram's desires and God's plans. In either case, God is saying that God is not God if the promise fails to be fulfilled.

But God is God. And the promise is fulfilled. Abram has his guarantee.

6 WILLFULNESS AND GRACE

Genesis 12:10-20 13:1-18; 16:1-16

LEARNING MENU

Based on what you know about your class members, their needs, and the ways in which they learn best, choose at least one learning activity from each of the Dimensions.

Dimension 1: What Does the Bible Say?

(A) Answer Dimension 1 questions.

Continue patiently to encourage class members to read the assigned Bible passages ahead of class and to work on the Dimension 1 questions. If they have not done so, allow some time to do so now.

- Discussion of the Dimension 1 questions may lead in these directions:
  1. The short answer to the question of how Sarai escaped from Pharaoh's harem is that *God made it happen*. The longer answer is that Pharaoh realized that Sarai was Abram's wife as well as his sister (actually, his *half* sister) when God inflicted him and his household with "great plagues."
     Some of today's readers might wonder why God punished Pharaoh with plagues when Pharaoh had acted out of innocence, or at least out of ignorance, when he took Sarai into his harem. Or perhaps some might wonder why Abram was not also punished. After all, he was perfectly willing to pass Sarai off as his sister and permit her to go into Pharaoh's harem if it meant his own survival.
     Although we today might question Abram's motives and morality in this story, the Bible text itself does not raise this issue. From the perspective of the writer and readers of this story, two points are important: (1) that God acted in order to preserve the integrity of the promise made to Abram; and (2) that the mighty Egyptian Empire suffered embarrassment for the sake of the lowly, powerless ancestors of Israel. The viewpoint of the text itself is that nothing is more important, nor more powerful, than God's covenant with Israel.
  2. In order to answer this question, try looking at a good map of Bible lands during the time of Abraham, such as may be found in many Bibles, in a Bible atlas, or in *Bible Teacher Kit* (Abingdon, 1994; available from Cokesbury). When Abram tells Lot to choose which land he wants, they are standing somewhere between Bethel and Ai. If your map shows the topography of the area, you will find that they are standing on the highest ridge between the Jordan River Valley and the Mediterranean Sea. Lot looks east and sees the moist fertility of the valley ("the plain of the Jordan"). He chooses the low country for

28 JOURNEY THROUGH THE BIBLE

himself and his descendants, the Moabites. The region across the Jordan River east of Jericho became known as the Plain of Moab. Traditionally, the southern portions of the Dead Sea are thought to cover the devastated cities of Sodom and Gomorrah, part of Lot's territory. Meanwhile, this agreement left Abram with the high, hill country of Canaan as his to settle.

3. Genesis 16:11-12 presents the message of the angel of the LORD to Hagar concerning Ishmael's destiny. There seem to be two main points to the message.
   —God cares for Ishmael in a special way. The name *Ishmael* literally means "God hears."
   —Ishmael will be wild, uncivilized, and hostile.
   The descendants of Ishmael turn out to be desert nomads. Muslim tradition holds that Ishmael was the ancestor of the Arabs.

(B) Chart the conflicts.

The three episodes examined in this chapter are essentially conflict stories. One way to help persons understand what happens and what is at stake in the conflict is to chart the dynamics in each episode.

- You will need newsprint or other writing surface and appropriate markers.
- Ahead of class time, prepare a chart outline on the newsprint or writing surface.
—Leaving the upper left hand corner blank, headings going across the top should list the three Bible passages for this chapter: GENESIS 12:10-20; GENESIS 13:1-18; GENESIS 16:1-16.
—Again leaving the same upper left hand corner blank, headings going down the left hand side should list the following headings: MAIN CHARACTERS; MAIN ACTION; SOURCE OF CONFLICT; THREAT TO THE COVENANT; RESOLUTION OF CONFLICT; MEANING FOR THE COVENANT.
- One way to work on the chart is to ask arriving class members to begin reading one of the three Bible passages and to fill in the portions on the chart for that passage. As other members arrive, they can be put to work on the other passages or to work with persons already working on a passage.
- Another way to work on the chart is for the entire class to read each of the three passages in sequence, working together to fill in the blanks on the chart.
- If you are using a large writing surface for your chart, such as a long chalkboard, yet another way to work on the chart would be to divide the class into three groups. Each group can work on filling in the chart after reading one assigned Bible passage.
- Whichever option you choose, allow time for the whole class to discuss the completed chart. In particular, encourage class members to discuss apparent similarities and differences among the three passages, especially regarding conflicts, resolutions, and their significance for the covenant.

Dimension 2: What Does the Bible Mean?

(C) Imagine Sarai's predicament.

- You will need to provide scratch paper and writing utensils for this learning activity.
- This is a learning activity you can ask persons to work on individually or as members of small groups of two or three persons. The size of your class and the learning styles and needs of its members will help you decide which way to lead this activity.
- Everyone will need to read or review Genesis 12:10-20, the episode in which Abram permits Pharaoh to take Sarai into his harem.
- Persons (or groups) will next work on developing first-person accounts of this episode. They may choose to tell the story from the point of view of
   —Sarai
   —Abram, or
   —Pharaoh
- Scratch paper may be used to jot down ideas, outlines, or a complete narrative.
- Invite persons (or groups) to share their created first-person narratives. Allow time for discussion.

(D) Research Abram's and Lot's lands.

- You will need to provide a variety of Bible atlases, Bible dictionaries, and Bible concordances. If your church has a library, you might want to have your class members undertake this learning activity there.
- Divide the class members into two groups. If your class is large, then divide the class into an even number of groups and assign each task to half the groups.
- Allow time for persons to read or review Genesis 13:1-18, the episode about Abram and Lot dividing up the land.
- One group (or half the groups in a larger class) is to find out everything it can about the land Lot chose. The other group (or the other half of the groups) is to find out everything it can about the land Abram chose.
- Allow time for groups to report and discuss their findings. Possible areas for groups to explore during their research and the subsequent discussion include the following questions:
—What can you say about the terrains Abram and Lot chose?

—What were the similarities and differences between the lands?
—Who were the peoples later found during Bible times in those lands? Who are the peoples found in those lands today?
—What are some of the major cities in those two lands, both in Bible times and today?
—What events does the Bible tell about that happened in those two lands?
—What might the terrain and resources found in those lands tell you about the type of life that would develop in those places?
—What does Lot's choice of land tell you about him?
—Who got the better deal in Lot's choice of land: Abram? or Lot? Why?

Some starting ideas might be found in the discussion above of Question 2 within Dimension 1 (see Learning Activity "A").

(E) Find out about Hagar and Ishmael.

- You will need to provide a variety of Bible dictionaries, commentaries, and concordances for use during this learning activity. If your church has a library, you might want to let the class do this learning activity there.
- Divide the class into work groups of three to five persons. Each group will have the same assignment: Find out all you can about Hagar and Ishmael.
- Allow ten to fifteen minutes for groups to carry out their research. Some groups may quickly learn that outside of Genesis 16:1-16, 17:18-27, and 21:9-21, there is not much information about Hagar or Ishmael.
- Persons who use a concordance should be cautioned that the persons named Ishmael mentioned in Second Kings, Jeremiah, and a few other places in the Old Testament are not the same person as the son of Abram and Hagar.
- After research has been completed, ask each group to settle on seven adjectives that best describe Hagar and seven adjectives that best describe Ishmael.
- After groups share and discuss their findings, you might also discuss
—What seemed to be Abram's attitude toward Hagar?
—What seemed to be Abram's attitude toward Ishmael?
—What evidence can you find of Ishmael's attitude toward Abram?
—To what extent do you think Hagar and Ishmael were dealt with justly?
—How would you retell the treatment of Hagar and Ishmael from Hagar's perspective?

Dimension 3:
What Does the Bible Mean to Us?

(F) Get out of God's way.

- If your class did Learning Activity "B" above, keep that chart visible as a source for reviewing the biblical material.
- Divide the class into three groups. If you have a large class, you might want to divide into six or nine groups (or some multiple of three) and assign each Bible text to one-third of the groups.
- Ask each group to read or review one of the Bible passages studied in this chapter:
—Genesis 12:10-20
—Genesis 13:1-18
—Genesis 16:1-16
- Using insights into the Bible passages they have already gained as well as their imaginations, ask group members to spend time imagining two things:
  1. What might have happened if human beings had not tried to act on their own in the episode you are examining? In other words, what might have happened, had Abram not insisted upon calling Sarai his sister instead of his wife, or even had Abram and Sarai not gone to Egypt in the first place? Or what might have happened, had Abram not tried to settle his quarrel with Lot by offering Lot his choice of land? Or what might have happened, had Sarai not offered Hagar to bear Abram's child?
  2. What might have happened in the episode you are examining had God not intervened? (The group considering the second episode will have to decide for themselves whether God intervened in Lot's choice of land, though the Bible says nothing on that matter.)

  Remind class members that their use of imagination should be playful. They can delve into what might have been even while they are well aware of what the biblical text says actually did happen.
- Allow time for groups to share and discuss their imaginings. Then discuss, in groups or in the class as a whole:
—In what ways do we thwart God by seeking to control our own situations and our own destinies?
—When ought we to do nothing rather than something in a situation? How do we know?
—To what extent does God act within the events of history, including current events?
—To what extent does God act within the events of personal experience?
—To what extent does God intervene when we cause predicaments by trying to control events and situations?
—To what extent does God rescue us from the predicaments we cause?

—What happens if God does not act to rescue us personally?

—In the story of Lot choosing his land, did God intervene or was Abram simply "lucky" that Lot left the promised land of Canaan for Abram's settlement?

(G) Discover another perspective on Ishmael.

- If your congregation is located near a Muslim population, you can try either of these approaches for this learning activity:

—You can ask for one or more volunteers to interview a Muslim; or

—You can invite a Muslim who is articulate to meet with your class for all or part of a class session.

- Within either approach, ask the following questions about the role of Ishmael within the Islamic understanding. You should provide a copy of Genesis 16:1-16, 17:18-27, and 21:9-21 beforehand to the person being interviewed and let him or her know in advance that you are wanting to know more about how Muslims understand Ishmael, Hagar, and Abraham.

—Who is Ishmael for the Muslims?

—How do Muslims understand and relate to Abraham?

—What does the Koran say about Abraham and Ishmael?

—Is there an understanding of a covenant from God within Islam?

—What is your understanding about the roles of Isaac and Ishmael in the sacrifice Abraham was asked to make of his son?

—How do Muslims understand their relationship to Jews and to Christians, especially with regard to a common heritage traced back to Abraham?

Additional Bible Helps

"The Grace of Doing Nothing"

This chapter's "Additional Bible Helps" are different from those appearing in other chapters of the leader's guide. Instead of providing additional material that bears on the original context of a Bible passage, this section serves as a modern reflection on the main theme of this chapter.

"The Grace of Doing Nothing" was written in 1932 by one of the greatest Christian theologians of this or any century, H. Richard Niebuhr. The article was written as an attempt to explore what, if anything, American Christians should do *as Christians* in response to the Japanese occupation of the Manchurian province of China. It was published in the March 23, 1932, issue of *The Christian Century*. Richard's equally famous and knowledgeable brother, Reinhold Niebuhr responded to Richard's conclusions in *The Christian Century* a week later with his own article, "Must We Do Nothing?" In the following week's issue, Richard offered a rejoinder with "A Communication: The Only Way Into the Kingdom of God."

You are invited to keep the three Bible passages assigned for this chapter in mind as you read the excerpts from H. Richard Niebuhr's "The Grace of Doing Nothing." As you do so, reflect upon the problems Abraham caused by trying to act when perhaps inaction was the more appropriate response.

We are not suggesting that H. Richard Niebuhr's position was the only proper Christian perspective in the decade prior to World War II. However, he does offer us one Christian perspective that gives us pause to ponder how we might apply the lessons of this chapter to our own lives as individuals, as a class and congregation, and as a society and nation.

"It may be that the greatest moral problems of the individual or of a society arise when there is nothing to be done. When we have begun a certain line of action or engaged in a conflict we cannot pause too long to decide which of various possible courses we ought to choose for the sake of the worthier result. Time rushes on and we must choose as best we can, entrusting the issue to the future. It is when we stand aside from the conflict, before we know what our relations to it really are, when we seem to be condemned to doing nothing, that our moral problems become greatest. How shall we do nothing?

"The issue is brought home to us by the fighting in the east. We are chafing at the bit, we are eager to do something constructive; but there is nothing constructive, it seems, that we can do. We pass resolutions, aware that we are doing nothing; we summon up righteous indignation and still do nothing; we write letters to congressmen and secretaries, asking others to act while we do nothing. Yet is it really true that we are doing nothing? There are, after all, various ways of being inactive and some kinds of inactivity, if not all, may be highly productive. It is not really possible to stand aside, to sit by the fire in this world of moving times; even Peter was doing something in the courtyard of the high-priest's house—if it was only something he was doing to himself. When we do nothing we are also affecting the course of history. The problem we face is often that of choice between various kinds of inactivity rather than of choice between action and inaction.

. . . .

"But there is another way of doing nothing. It appears to be highly impracticable because it rests on the well-nigh obsolete faith that there is a God—a real God. Those who follow this way share . . . the belief that the fact that men can do nothing constructive is no indication of the fact that nothing constructive is being done. . . . [T]hey are assured that the actual processes of history will inevitably and really bring a different kind of world with lasting peace. They do not rely on human aspirations after ideals to accomplish this end, but on forces which often seem very impersonal—as impersonal as those which eliminated slavery in spite of the abolitionists. The forces may be as impersonal and as actual as machine production, rapid transportation, the physical mixture of the races, etc., but as parts of the real world they are as much a part of the total divine process as are human thoughts and prayers.

. . . .

"This way of doing nothing the old Christians called repentance, but the word has become so reminiscent of emotional debauches in the feeling of guilt that it may be better to abandon it for a while. What is suggested is that the only effective approach to the problem of China and Japan lies in the sphere of an American self-analysis which is likely to result in some surprising discoveries as to the amount of renunciation of self-interest necessary on the part of this country and of individual Christians before anything effective can be done in the east.

". . . It is not the inactivity of a resigned patience, but of a patience that is full of hope, and is based on faith. . . .

"But if there is no God, or if God is up in heaven and not in time itself, it is a very foolish inactivity."

(From "The Grace of Doing Nothing," by H. Richard Niebuhr. Copyright 1932 Christian Century Foundation. Reprinted by permission from the March 23, 1932 issue of *The Christian Century*.)

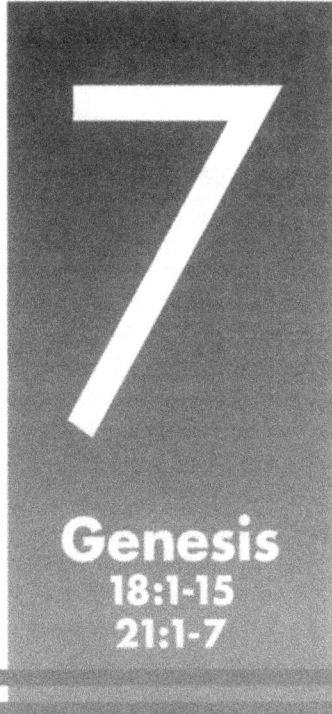

7 HOSPITALITY AND LAUGHTER

Genesis 18:1-15
21:1-7

LEARNING MENU
Based on what you know about your class members, their needs, and the ways in which they learn best, choose at least one learning activity from each of the three Dimensions.

Dimension 1: What Does the Bible Say?

(A) Answer Dimension 1 questions.

- If class members have not worked on Dimension 1 questions yet, provide a limited amount of time during which they may read the assigned Bible passages and answer the questions. Be sure, though, to reserve plenty of time to get into the other two dimensions.
- Discussion of Dimension 1 questions may lead in these directions. Keep in mind that some questions may have straightforward answers while others may involve more than one way to answer or open themselves up to discussion.
  1. In Genesis 18:1-15, Abraham and Sarah offer the strangers
     —water to wash the dirt off their feet;
     —a place under a tree to rest out of the hot sun;
     —a meal—better than the "little bread" Abraham had offered—made of at least a calf ("tender and good"), curds, milk, and cakes made of "choice flour";
     —Abraham's personal attention as they sat eating;
     —no apparent expectation of anything in return.
  2. Sarah laughed in Genesis 18 because she found it impossibly ludicrous that at her advanced, menopausal age anyone should say that before long she would conceive a child. She knew there was no physical way she could bear the child that the stranger said she would be bearing.
  3. Sarah's laughter in Genesis 21 stems from a joy that in Genesis 18 she never thought possible to have—the joy of giving birth to a child. Note two further points about Sarah's laughter here:
     —Sarah recognizes that this laughter comes from God's activity.
     —Sarah considers God's action to cause her to bear a child to be so great that everyone who hears about it will laugh with delight.

(B) Write the text into a dramatic play.

- Divide your class into groups of four to six persons.
- Allow time for each group to read through Genesis 18:1-15 and 21:1-7.
- Give each group the same task of turning these two Bible passages into a dramatic play. As they work on

HOSPITALITY AND LAUGHTER 33

writing their plays, encourage them to consider the following:
- What type of play will they write based on these passages: a drama? a comedy? a tragedy?
- What is the main plot line?
- Are there any subplots?
- How many acts and scenes should there be?
- What characters inhabit the play? Which are main characters? Which characters have supporting roles? What are the personalities and distinguishing features of each of the characters?
- What are the settings for the various scenes? If you were able to do it up right, what would you need for props and costumes?
- After you write the lines and talk about how you would block out the action (that is, who would do what when during the play), how should the lines be delivered and with what kind of inflection?
- Once groups have worked on developing their plays, you have several options for what to do next:
- You can ask groups to describe what their play would be like.
- You can ask groups to perform all or part of their play.
- You can ask one group to start its play, stop the action at a crucial point, and ask another group to pick up the action from there according to *its* play.
- A more tame but briefer alternative to asking groups to write and perform their own play is to use the Bible text itself as a dramatic reading:
- You will need volunteers to read the following parts:
  - Narrator;
  - Abraham;
  - Sarah;
  - The LORD (who is either alone or included among the three strange men, depending upon how you read the text).
- You will need each reader to read from the same translation of the Bible, such as the New Revised Standard Version. Remember that the assigned text includes both Genesis 18:1-15 and 21:1-7.
- Each character reads the words attributed in the text to that character. The narrator reads everything not in quotation marks.
- Allow a brief amount of time for readers to read over and become familiar with their lines. Encourage them to decide how they will use inflection in their voices so that it sounds like what their character might really have said.
- Whichever way you choose to dramatize these texts, be sure to allow time for the class to discuss what they learned from studying the text in this way.

Dimension 2: What Does the Bible Mean?

(C) Share examples of excellence in hospitality.

The hospitality illustrated by Abraham and Sarah in Genesis 18:1-8 is often cited as a prime example of the best in hospitality practiced in the ancient Near East. Read or review that passage so that class members gain a taste for what the Old Testament understood as excellence in hospitality. You may also wish to read or summarize the information in the sidebar entitled, "The Moral Imperative of Hospitality," page 56 in the study book.

- As a whole class or in smaller groups, ask persons to share their own contemporary examples of excellence in hospitality. The study book, in the section on "Excellence in Hospitality" (pages 57-58), offers some examples with which to start, such as hotels with certain amenities and Disney World.
- You might try one of two methods for the sharing of examples:
- In "popcorning," persons simply call out their examples as they think of them, something like a kernel of popcorn that seems spontaneously to pop when it is ready.
- In a "round robin," persons share one idea at a time in turn as you go around the group. Persons are allowed to pass without saying anything at anytime if they wish. You can go around the group only once, a limited number of times around the group, or around the group as many times as necessary in order to exhaust the examples every person has.
- After sharing examples, discuss:
- What kinds of features do these examples of excellence in hospitality share in common?
- What effect does hospitality seem to have on persons? Why?
- In what ways do you think hospitality is a "moral imperative"?
- In what ways is the hospitality that Christians are to practice similar or different from the examples of excellence in hospitality you have mentioned?
- How should *Christian* hospitality be practiced?
- What would be the features of examples of excellence in *Christian* hospitality?
- What are some specific ways by which your class or your congregation might increase its excellence in practicing Christian hospitality?

(D) Meditate on an icon.

A black-and-white reproduction of Rublev's famous 1411 icon, "The Holy Trinity," may be found on page 55 of the study book. You may be able to find a color reproduction in a book of icons or in a book of Russian art.

An icon is used in personal and congregational worship within the tradition of the Orthodox Church. It is a picture painted according to a very stringent set of rules by an artist who is spiritually devout as well as artistically skilled. Rather than being a representation of what the artist sees or visualizes in his or her mind's eye, an icon seeks to present a picture as if it were from the perspective of eternity. One thing this means is that although icons are usually very intentionally symmetrical, they do not have the sense of perspective Western paintings usually have. That is because they are not intended to be "viewed" from the point of view of the viewer outside of the picture. The "vanishing point" that gives Western paintings their depth is not present in the icon. Rather the "vanishing point" is situated where the outside viewer stands. Within the Orthodox tradition, icons serve a function as somewhat of a "spiritual friend" rather than as an object of worship.

- For more background information on icons, one good source is *The Icon: Windows of the Kingdom*, by Michel Quenot, St. Vladimir's Seminary Press, 1991.
- After summarizing some background information about icons in general and Rublev's icon of "The Holy Trinity" in particular, ask class members to look at either the study book's reproduction or at a color reproduction if you have been able to obtain one. Tell them that earlier generations of Christians have puzzled over the way the LORD and the three men seem to blend into each other in Genesis 18. One way Christians have resolved their puzzle in a way that is not directly supported by a strict reading of the text is to say that the three men really are God as the Trinity: the Father, the Son, and the Holy Spirit.
- Ask class members to look at the icon as you read Genesis 18:1-15. Afterward discuss these questions:
—What did you experience as you looked at the icon while hearing the Scripture passage on which it was based?
—Did you notice anything about either the Scripture passage or the icon you had not noticed before until they were put together?
—What do you think or feel about the icon's depiction of the three men as the Holy Trinity?

Dimension 3:
What Does the Bible Mean to Us?

(E) Fall over laughing.

- Read or re-read the three moments of laughter in this part of Genesis:
  —Genesis 17:15-18 (Abraham laughs);
  —Genesis 18:9-15 (Sarah laughs);
  —Genesis 21:6-7 (God and all the world laughs with Sarah).
- Note how in the Genesis 17 passage, verse 17 says that "Then Abraham fell on his face and laughed, and said to himself, 'Can a child be born to a man who is a hundred years old? Can Sarah, who is ninety years old, bear a child?'" Not only did Abraham laugh, but Abraham laughed so hard that he fell down laughing!
- Discuss:
—What would make you laugh so hard that you actually might fall down laughing?
—What do you think caused Abraham's laughter in this case?
—What qualities do you think were present in Abraham's character that enabled him to laugh so hard? to laugh so hard in God's presence? to laugh so hard at something God had told him?
- If your class members are comfortable doing so, ask them to demonstrate laughing. In a "round robin" manner, each person might demonstrate a different type of laughter. For example, different types of laughing might include giggles, chuckles, snickers, "sound track" laughter, and belly laughs. Talk about the different circumstances that might bring forth each different type of laughter.
- Another possibility would be to read each of the three passages listed above in which laughter occurs. After each passage, ask volunteers to give their rendition of the type of laughter described in the context of that passage. For example, ask volunteers to demonstrate the type of laughter that might cause Abraham to fall down laughing in Genesis 17. If more than one volunteer is available for each laugh (and hopefully there will be), invite the other class members to judge which laugh demonstration best fits that passage.
- Discuss:
—What happens to you physically when you laugh? mentally? emotionally? spiritually?
—When in your religious life might you laugh?
—Under what circumstances do you think or feel laughter might be appropriate within the context of worship?
—How open is your congregation to the possibility of laughter as a spiritual experience?
—How might laughter become a part of your prayer life?
- You might close out this segment of your class session by noting that there will be laughter in God's Kingdom if we believe Jesus' statement: "Blessed are you who weep now, for you will laugh" (Luke 6:21b).

(F) Look at the doubt behind belief.

- If you have not done Learning Activity "E" above involving laughter, read Genesis 17:15-18 (in which Abraham laughs) and Genesis 18:9-15 (in which Sarah

HOSPITALITY AND LAUGHTER

35

laughs). In any case, note that at least part of the motives behind Abraham's and Sarah's laughing fits were that they found God's statements to them about a child to be utterly ridiculous. They were so absurd as to be "laughable."
- Discuss:
—Why do you think Sarah denied laughing in Genesis 18:15?
—To what extent did their laughter demonstrate that Abraham and Sarah did not believe God's promise of a child?
—Granted that Abraham and Sarah are often held up as the highest examples of faith, as in Romans 4 and in Hebrews 6 and 11, what do the occasions of laughter on the part of Abraham and Sarah teach about the place of *doubt* or *unbelief* within faith?
—How much faith in God is enough faith?
—How much doubt is allowable in a person's attempt to have faith in God?
- One option for adding to this learning activity would be to invite persons privately to write down or to draw their personal belief-to-disbelief ratios.
—You will need scratch paper and writing/drawing utensils for each person. Some persons may prefer to use colored markers or crayons.
—Invite persons to reflect privately on the amount of disbelief or doubt compared to the amount of belief present in their lives at the moment.
—After distributing paper and writing/drawing utensils, permit persons to move where they want in the room if they desire privacy. Ask them to write or draw some representation of the ratio of belief to disbelief/unbelief/doubt in their lives.
- You might want to close out this segment of the class session, or the class session itself if this is the last part of it, with a "breath prayer."
—Invite class members to sit comfortably, with both feet on the floor, hands resting in their laps, and eyes closed.
—Ask persons to concentrate on the rhythm of their breathing, as they breathe in and out slowly.
—As they become comfortable with the rhythm of their breathing, invite them to add silently to the rhythm of their breathing over and over the rhythmic prayer: *Lord, I believe. Help my unbelief.*

Additional Bible Helps

A Story of Laughter
"I had really given up all hope of having children, that day those three strangers came to our tent. I was inside, tending to my household chores, so I didn't see them coming. Actually, Abraham said he'd not seen them coming, either. They just sort of materialized—three men, just standing there, at a little distance from the door of the tent.

"Perhaps he sensed there was something special about them. Or maybe it was just our Hebrew hospitality. But he rushed up to them, invited them to stay a while, to wash their feet, rest under the tree, have a little food.

"They agreed. He ran in to tell me to make some bread, and he got meat for them and some milk and butter and brought out the food and set it before them.

"They ate. No big surprises, so far.

"But then . . . I was still inside the tent—out of sight, you understand—resting after the rush to get food ready, enjoying the hum of voices, when I heard one of them say, 'Where's your wife? Sarah?'

"They knew my name! Abraham hadn't told them. I certainly hadn't. I'd done my best to keep out of their way. Even if they'd seen me, how would they know my name?

"Abraham was dumbfounded, too. But he just said, 'She's in the tent.'

"Then the one who seemed to be the leader made the most astonishing statement. In the first place, it was an odd subject to bring up about a virtual stranger. In the second place, he might have guessed that Abraham, as old as he was, would have a wife who was no spring chicken. Although, of course, lots of men do marry younger women—but *that* much younger?

"Anyway, this fellow said, 'Your wife is going to have a son.'

"*Oh sure,* I thought. *Come on, guys.* You could have knocked me over with a feather. In the first place, it's none of a stranger's business to be speculating about the reproductive life of people he doesn't even know. And in the second place I'd passed through menopause years ago! *No way am I going to get pregnant at my age,* I thought.

"So I laughed to myself. Now this is important. I laughed to myself. Didn't open my mouth. Didn't make a peep. Didn't stifle a chuckle. To myself I laughed. I was inside the tent, so he couldn't even have seen a smile pass over my face.

"Well, the man was a mind reader, because he says, to Abraham, 'How come your wife laughed? She thinks she's too old to have a baby? Is anything impossible with God?'

"*With God?* I thought. *What is this? And who is this stranger who knows my name and sees into my heart to know that I laughed—and then make the preposterous suggestion?*

"This time I didn't laugh, let me tell you. I was afraid. That fellow might have thought I'd been rude, and what other power might he have? I stepped to the doorway of the tent. 'I didn't laugh,' I said, my voice trembling.

" 'Yes, you did,' he said. 'I'll come back again. You'll see. By the time I come back, you'll have that son.'

"They left. I was glad to see them go. But shaken, too.

"Abraham and I sat down and talked about it. Was this visitor a seer? Did he know something we didn't know? To become parents at our age?

"It had been very painful to us that we couldn't conceive a child. We'd been married young. At first I was in no hurry. I don't think he was either. We were having a lot of fun, just the two of us. Time enough for children when we were a little older, more ready to settle down.

"But we did nothing to prevent my getting pregnant, either, and after a few years we began to wonder—was there something wrong? We consulted doctors. We tried folk remedies. But nothing happened. After many years we gave up, resigned ourselves to childlessness, spent time with our nieces and nephews, the other children of the tribe.

"But the heartache stayed. So that, old as I was, even behind my laughter—my *silent* laughter—was a tiny leap of hope. Crazy as it seemed, could it be so? Could that stranger be right? The one who knew my name, who heard my silent laughter?"

She tips her head and laughs, careful not to jostle the baby in her arms. "Now God has given me joy, to laugh aloud!" She holds up the baby for the visitor to see—"Look at him. Isaac," she murmurs against the baby's downy cheek.

(By Martha Whitmore Hickman. From *The Storyteller's Companion to the Bible*, Volume Four, "Old Testament Women," edited by Michael E. Williams. Copyright © 1993 by Abingdon Press. Used by permission.)

Sodom and Gomorrah

Genesis 18:16–19:29

LEARNING MENU
Keeping in mind the ways in which your class members learn best as well as their needs and interests, choose at least one learning segment from each of the three Dimensions.

Dimension 1: What Does the Bible Say?

(A) Discuss Dimension 1 questions.

- If many class members have not yet read the Bible text for this session, nor have worked on responses to the Dimension 1 questions, allow a limited amount of time for them to do so now.
- Discussion of Dimension 1 questions may move in the following directions:
  1. In Genesis 18:22-33, Abraham's attempts to persuade God not to destroy Sodom have at least two major dynamics at work:
     —Verse 25 implies that to destroy righteous persons along with the wicked is incompatible with God's character: "Shall not the Judge of all the earth do what is just?"
     —Abraham then nudges God's tolerance threshhold downward notch by notch so that instead of a critical mass of fifty righteous persons being enough to save the whole city, by the end of the passage God is willing to preserve Sodom for the sake of only ten righteous persons. By the way, it is interesting to note in verse 33 that after agreeing to preserve Sodom for the sake of ten righteous persons, God breaks off the discussion first. We might speculate that God was unwilling to bargain any further with Abraham that day!
  2. Genesis 19 begins the story of Lot's hospitality that compares roughly with the story of Abraham's and Sarah's hospitality in Genesis 18:1-9, though with some differences:
     —Instead of encountering the men/angels near his tent as Abraham did, Lot was sitting at the gateway entering into Sodom. One immediate difference is that although Abraham apparently still was a nomad living in tents, Lot had become a city dweller within Sodom.
     —Abraham ran to meet his visitors; Lot only rose to meet them, though both bowed low to the ground in humble greeting.
     —Lot offered a night's lodging along with refreshment. To that extent, Lot offered something that Abraham had not offered.
     —The visitors were initially unwilling to accept Lot's hospitality until he urged them strongly to

stay with him rather than bedding down in the town square.
—The only item mentioned in the "feast" Lot served was unleavened bread.
—Lot was willing to go to the extraordinary means of surrendering his daughters to a mob for the sake of preserving the safety of the two visitors to whom he had promised lodging.

3. Although modern Christians may quarrel with Lot's willingness to expose his daughters to sexual abuse for the sake of keeping the strangers safe from similar harm, that action demonstrated a certain moral strength within Lot's character. He was willing to go to extreme sacrifices for the sake of the virtue of hospitality. (One may rightfully argue that the sacrifice would actually have been given by Lot's daughters. They are the ones who would have suffered; not Lot. However, within the cultural perspective of that time and place, Lot's daughters were in a sense his property. They did not have a real life of their own.)

4. Reading the text carefully, three persons ultimately survive the destruction of Sodom: Lot and his two daughters. Lot's wife, of course, looks back and becomes a pillar of salt. Lot's sons-in-law, "who were to marry his daughters," thought Lot was joking and stayed behind in the city to be destroyed.

(B) Evaluate the characters of Abraham and Lot.

- You will need a large writing surface, such as a white board, chalkboard, or newsprint, along with appropriate markers or chalk. You will also need to provide persons with scratch paper and writing utensils as they arrive.
- As persons arrive, ask them to draw a line down the center of the scratch paper you have given them. Then ask them to list all the qualities of character they can for Abraham on one half and all the qualities of character for Lot on the other. They may draw upon anything they know about the lives of Abraham and Lot. They should include information from this session's Bible text, Genesis 18:16–19:29.
- After you have called persons together to begin class, ask each person in turn to share one quality of character for Abraham while you write it on the large writing surface. Continue around the group until everyone has exhausted his or her list. Then do the same sharing of qualities of character for Lot.
- Allow time for discussion regarding particular qualities of character as well as about the type of persons Abraham and Lot were once one puts together all the qualities of character listed for them.

Dimension 2: What Does the Bible Mean?

(C) Examine the reputations of Sodom and Gomorrah.

- You may want to have on hand a variety of Bible reference tools such as Bible dictionaries, concordances, and one-volume commentaries.
- Note that throughout the Bible, the cities of Sodom and Gomorrah are used as illustrations of unrepentant evil as well as of what happens when God's wrath falls. Sodom is first mentioned in Genesis 13, when Lot chooses to settle in the plain of the Jordan River, which at that time was a flourishing pastureland. Yet even as Lot settles among the cities of the Plain, a warning about Sodom is already there: "Now the people of Sodom were wicked, great sinners against the LORD" (Genesis 13:13).
- Assign one or more of the following passages to individuals or groups. Each of these passages states something about the reputations of Sodom and Gomorrah:
  —Deuteronomy 29:10-29
  —Isaiah 1:7-11
  —Jeremiah 23:9-15
  —Ezekiel 16:43-58
  —Matthew 10:5-15
  —Luke 10:1-12
  —Romans 9:19-29
  —2 Peter 2:1-10
  —Jude 5-7
  —Revelation 11:7-8
- Persons or groups should study their assigned passages. Using available Bible reference tools, they should try to answer these questions about each passage:
—What is actually being said about Sodom and/or Gomorrah in this passage?
—How does what is said about Sodom and/or Gomorrah fit in with the argument or narrative within which this briefer passage fits? In other words, what is the context of this passage about Sodom and/or Gomorrah?
—Who is writing these words? (Information about authors of the books of the Bible, as well as other helpful information may often be found in brief articles some editions of the Bible place at the start of each book of the Bible. Another good source is at the beginning of the material for a particular book of the Bible within one-volume commentaries.)
—To whom are these passages addressed? Why might they be addressed to these particular audiences?
—What is being warned about? (Read the text in and around the stated passage to see what, if anything, is specifically being warned about. Do not simply assume

you know what is being warned about without reading the Bible text carefully.)
—What comparisons are being made using Sodom and/or Gomorrah?
• Provide time to share and discuss findings as a whole class.
• Discuss:
—What did you learn about the reputations of Sodom and Gomorrah during Bible times?
—What similarities and differences did you find among these passages?

(D) Note the difference that a footnote can make.

This learning segment looks at one verse and the footnote attached to that verse within many versions of the Bible. You might want to have several versions of the Bible available. This learning segment also teaches an often overlooked aspect of studying a particular Bible text closely.

• Ask persons to note what version of the Bible they are using, such as the New Revised Standard Version, the New International Version, the *Good News Bible*, and so forth. In order to make sure there are a variety of different Bible versions being used for this segment, you may wish to distribute Bibles you have on hand for this purpose.
• Invite persons using different Bible versions to read aloud Genesis 18:22. Ask readers to check the verse for evidence of a footnote. If a footnote is associated with Genesis 18:22 in their version, ask them to locate that footnote in a side or bottom margin and to read it aloud.
—For example, the main text for Genesis 18:22 in the New Revised Standard Version reads: "So the men turned from there, and went toward Sodom, while Abraham remained standing before the LORD." However, the footnote associated with that verse states: "Another ancient tradition reads *while the LORD remained standing before Abraham*."
—For another example, the main text for that verse in *The Revised English Bible* reads: "When the men turned and went off towards Sodom, Abraham remained standing before the LORD." A footnote to that verse reads: "*original reading was probably* the LORD remained standing before Abraham."
—Some Bible versions, such as the *Good News Bible*, do not list any footnotes to this verse.
—For more information about footnotes and text variations, class members may wish to read introductions and other relevant articles that appear in the front of many Bibles.
• Discuss:
—What differences might this footnote make for understanding the meaning of Genesis 18:22? (Encourage class members to play around with different ideas rather than trying immediately to settle on one supposedly "right" answer.)
—From reading introductory material and other articles in the front of your Bible, what appears to be the reason why Bible translators believed this footnote to be necessary? In other words, why is there more than one translation, variation, or tradition in this Bible text?
—Which reading makes more sense to you: that Abraham remained standing before the LORD, or that the LORD remained standing before Abraham? Why?

(E) Consider Lot's values.

As has been noted, we modern readers and hearers of the story of Sodom and Gomorrah are shocked by Lot's willingness to sacrifice his daughters for the sake of the safety of the two strangers. If we get hung up on this point alone, however, we will miss other aspects the story has to offer.

• Allow time for persons to read or review Genesis 18:16–19:29.
• As you make a list on a large writing surface such as a white board, chalkboard, or newsprint, ask class members to name the values Lot seems to hold dear or to embody within this story.
• After a list is made, discuss:
—How did Lot's values set him apart from the other inhabitants of Sodom?
—What values seemed to count the most for Lot?

Dimension 3: What Does the Bible Mean to Us?

(F) Imagine wastelands of inhospitality.

• You will need to have a variety of magazines with photographs that may be cut out. You will also need enough pairs of scissors for each person to have a pair.
• In addition, you will need one or more Bible concordances and Bible atlases. You will also need copies of your church's hymnal.
• Review or summarize the material in "The Wasteland of Inhospitality," pages 67–68 in the study book.
• Invite persons to investigate the image of "the wasteland of inhospitality." Several learning options may be made available to persons to choose from depending on their own interests and learning styles:
—Some persons may choose to conduct a study of the image of wasteland as it appears in the Bible. One way to do this would be to discover where words such as *wasteland* and *desert* appear in the Bible. Discover:
—How are these words used as images?

—Are they used in one part of the Bible more than in another? Why does that appear to be?

—What happens in the wastelands and the deserts of the Bible?

- Some persons may choose to browse through magazines and cut out pictures that portray for them the image of "the wasteland of inhospitality."

- Some persons may choose to scan through the words of hymns in your church's hymnals that use imagery about deserts and wastelands. Discover:

—What kinds of hymns use desert and wasteland imagery?

—Are these hymns based on a particular part of the Bible?

—In what ways are desert and wasteland imagery used and resolved?

- Allow time for persons to share and discuss their findings from their explorations.

(G) Ponder some unanswerable questions.

- Review or summarize the material in "Attempting to Persuade God," page 66 in the study book.
- Discuss one or more of these questions raised within that section:

—Does God change God's mind?

—Is God's will eternally changeless?

—If God's will is changeless, was Abraham simply reminding God of some things that God might have forgotten?

—In our descriptions of God as all-knowing, were Abraham's pleadings with God redundant and irrelevant?

—Did Abraham insult God by implying that God was open to persuasion?

—Had God not already thought about the few righteous persons in Sodom before God planned to destroy the city?

—Had God been planning to destroy Lot along with everyone else in Sodom?

—What do you think about trying to persuade God or about trying to change God's mind?

Additional Bible Helps

Sodom and Homosexuality

A major, traditional strain of Christian biblical interpretation has associated the wickedness of Sodom, in particular, with homosexuality. This interpretation is grounded in the description of the attempted homosexual gang rape in Genesis 19:4-11. Of all the other biblical passages that mention the reputation for wickedness and God's judgment upon Sodom and Gomorrah, only Jude 7 specifically ties Sodom's sin directly to homosexuality: "Likewise, Sodom and Gomorrah and the surrounding cities, which, in the same manner as they, indulged in sexual immorality and pursued unnatural lust, serve as an example by undergoing a punishment of eternal fire."

Evidence of this traditional interpretation can be seen in the word *sodomy*, which came into usage within the English language sometime around the thirteenth century. "Anal intercourse and allied practices were known in late Latin as *peccātum Sodomīticum*, 'sin of Sodom,' and from this was coined the medieval Latin term *sodomia*—whence English *sodomy*. The abusive *sod* is short for the related *sodomite*" (from *Dictionary of Word Origins*, by John Ayto; Arcade Publishing, 1990; page 487).

An interpretation of the wickedness of Sodom that differs from this traditional interpretation is contained in this passage by Bible scholar Victor Paul Furnish:

Genesis 19:1-25: Lot's visitors and the men of Sodom (in Judg. 19, another version is told about Gibeah). Lot has offered lodging in his home to two strangers (who are actually angels in disguise). When the men of the city come to Lot's door demanding to have sex with his visitors, Lot offers them his virgin daughters instead. Even though the ruffians are not agreeable to his offer, Lot's guests manage to escape unharmed. The subsequent destruction of Sodom and Gomorrah is interpreted as God's judgment against the evil designs of Lot's neighbors.

This story is not told to condemn homosexuality, or even sexual lust in general, for in that case the story could not implicitly commend Lot's offering of his virgin daughters, which it does. The narrator's silence about this offer shows also his overall patriarchal viewpoint. Clearly, this story condemns those who violate the right of any stranger to be provided hospitality—a tradition deeply rooted in the culture of the ancient Near East. Although this particular violation would have involved same-sex rape, that is incidental to the main point.

Eventually, Sodom did come to symbolize same-sex acts—hence the later coining of the words *sodomy* and *Sodomites*. But despite their appearance in some English translations, these terms are never employed in the Bible itself. In the Bible, Sodom is only a symbol of evil in general, and for the judgment that will be visited upon all who continue in it (thus Ezek. 16:49-50).

(From "What Does the Bible Say About Homosexuality?" by Victor Paul Furnish, in *Caught in the Crossfire: Helping Christians Debate Homosexuality*, edited by Sally B. Geis and Donald E. Messer; Abingdon Press, 1994; pages 59–60.)

The R-Rated Bible

The story of the attempted homosexual gang rape in Sodom is a starkly ugly story. We may be appalled at the violence, at the homosexuality, at the violation of Lot's promised hospitality, or at Lot's proposed solution of giving his daughters over to the lust of the mob. If the story were graphically portrayed by Hollywood on the silver screen, doubtless the resulting movie would be given an "R" rating, recommending viewing by restricted audiences under age eighteen only if accompanied by a parent or guardian.

The ignominy of Sodom is sadly not the only story contained in the Bible that ought to be rated "R." For example, immediately following the story of Lot's escape from the destruction of Sodom comes the tale of how Lot's two daughters got Lot drunk and became pregnant through incest with him.

I can recall one adult Sunday school class I once taught that was packed for the session when the announced lesson was on David and Bathsheba. A session the following month was equally packed as we moved from lurid sex to graphic violence. The curriculum led us to study 2 Kings 9 and the story of the death of Queen Jezebel in which, after she was thrown from a window and the horses trampled her and the dogs got done with her, no more than her skull, her feet, and the palms of her hands could be found.

Many persons are astonished to find such stories in the Bible. Yet one thing we must say is that the Bible is filled with earthy, even tawdry, stories that reflect real life. Violence, the violation of persons, and harmful manifestations of sexuality do exist tragically in our world. The Bible does not shelter us from these tragedies.

The point is that we should not shrink from these stories, even if we are amazed that such stories should appear in the Holy Bible. While perhaps these stories should not be studied at every age level, adults cannot ignore them in a *mature* study of the Bible.

SACRIFICE

9

Genesis 22:1-19

LEARNING MENU
Keeping in mind the ways in which your class members learn best as well as their needs and interests, choose at least one learning segment from each of the three Dimensions.

Dimension 1: What Does the Bible Say?

(A) Discuss Dimension 1 questions.

- If many of your class members have not yet worked on the Dimension 1 questions, then allow a limited amount of time during class for persons to read or review Genesis 22:1-19 and to develop answers to the Dimension 1 questions.
- As mentioned in previous chapters, your class members will be best served if you do not permit the Dimension 1 questions to become the focus of your class sessions. Although learning the basic information of what the Bible actually says is important, it may be yet more important to move beyond the bare words of the text to learn what the Bible may actually have *meant* to its early readers and hearers, as well as to discern what the Bible means for you and your congregation.

- Discussion of Dimension 1 questions may lead in these directions:
  1. Incredibly, Genesis 22:2 says that God told Abraham, "Take your son, your only son Isaac, whom you love, and go to the land of Moriah, and offer him there as a burnt offering on one of the mountains that I shall show you." There is no avoiding the fact that God commanded Abraham to ritually slaughter his son, Isaac, and burn his flesh on an altar.
  2. As far as we can tell from the words of the biblical text, Abraham responded to God's command by setting out to do exactly that which God had said for him to do. There is no evidence from the text that Abraham hesitated or wavered. The text describes in some detail the steps Abraham went through to follow God's instructions precisely, even to the point of building an altar, preparing the wood for the burnt offering, laying Isaac (who is referred to as a "boy" but is of an unspecified age in this story) on the altar, and reaching out with his knife to kill Isaac.
  3. God responded by stopping the sacrifice before Isaac could be killed. God reassured Abraham that God noted Abraham's willingness even to surrender to God the child through whom the covenantal promise of vast descendants was to be fulfilled. Moreover, God provided a ram to substitute as a suitable sacrifice in Isaac's place.

43

4. God reiterated his previous promises to Abraham:
   —numerous (even innumerable) offspring;
   —those offspring will enjoy conquest of land and cities;
   —those same offspring will be the vehicle for all the nations of the world to receive blessing.

(B) Prepare a Father's Day card.

- You will need to provide construction paper in a variety of colors, scissors, magazines that may be cut up, glue, and markers or crayons.
- As class members arrive, ask them to read Genesis 22:1-19.
- Then instruct them to create Father's Day cards that Isaac might have made or picked out to give to his father, Abraham. If persons ask, they may choose whether Isaac is observing Father's Day before or after the day Abraham attempted to sacrifice him.
- Upon completion, invite persons to share their Father's Day card creations.
- Discuss:
—What kind of feelings do you think Isaac had about almost being a sacrifice slaughtered and burned as an offering to God?
—What kind of feelings do you think Isaac had toward his father, Abraham, before and after the almost-sacrifice?
—Do you think Isaac's relationship with Abraham changed because of the almost-sacrifice? If so, in what ways?
—Do you think Isaac struggled against the ropes that bound him to the altar when he saw his father approaching him with the knife?
—Do you think Abraham would have followed through all the way with the sacrifice, even to the point of plunging his knife into Isaac's throat?
—Do you think God was prepared to permit Abraham to go all the way through with sacrificing Isaac?

Dimension 2:
What Does the Bible Mean?

(C) Research the Jewish practice of sacrifice.

- You will need to provide a quantity and variety of Bible reference books, such as Bible dictionaries, concordances, and commentaries, that will offer information about the practice of sacrifice within the Jewish religion. If your church has a library, you might want to hold this part of the class session there.
- The "Additional Bible Helps" include excerpts on the topic of sacrifice from *The Religious World of Jesus: An Introduction to Second Temple Palestinian Judaism*, by Frederick J. Murphy (Abingdon Press, 1991). If you have access to that book, you will want to have it available for class use.
- Ask class members individually or in teams to research the topic of *sacrifice*. You might tell them they have twenty minutes in which to learn everything they can about the Jewish practice of sacrifice.
- As they research this topic, some of the questions they might consider include:
—What did the Hebrews or Jews who lived before the time of Jesus understand by the practice of sacrifice?
—Why did Jews sacrifice?
—What kinds of things did Jews sacrifice?
—What are a few key Old Testament passages that talk about sacrifice?
—What were the best things in your opinion that the Jewish practice of sacrifice had to offer?
—What were the worst things in your opinion that the Jewish practice of sacrifice had to offer?
—What did Jews apparently believe occurred during the carrying out of a sacrifice?
—Given that the almost-sacrifice of Isaac occurred before the sacrificial system of Israel was established, how do you think Abraham proposed to carry out that sacrifice?
—For what purposes did Jews practice sacrifice?
—Why do you think Abraham was prepared to carry out the sacrifice of Isaac?
- Allow time for persons to share and discuss their findings.

(D) Play the "What If" game.

- If class members have not yet done so, make sure they have time to read or review Genesis 22:1-19.
- In small groups or with the class as a whole, discuss the following hypothetical, "what if" questions. Keep in mind that hypothetical questions are "make believe" questions. They ponder things that never actually happened, wondering what might have happened if some event had been different in some way. As such, there are no "right" answers. They encourage persons to stretch their imaginations and think about what might have been. By doing so, persons will gain an understanding of some of the concerns that were at stake in the actual situation as it played itself out.
- Do not feel limited by the "what if" questions suggested here. Add your own that seem relevant to the text.
- Discuss these "what if" questions and others as you determine:
—What might have happened if Abraham had said no to God, that he would not take Isaac to the land of Moriah for the purpose of sacrificing him?
—What might have happened if one of the young men (who were probably servants) Abraham had taken with

him to help had figured out what Abraham's intent was, had moral qualms about it, and attempted to prevent Abraham from sacrificing Isaac?
—What might have happened if Isaac had figured out that he was supposed to be the sacrificial offering and had tried to escape that fate?
—What might have happened if God's angel had not stopped Abraham's knife?
—What might have happened if God had not provided a ram in the bushes to serve as a substitute in the sacrifice?
—What if Muslim tradition were correct and Ishmael was the son whom Abraham almost sacrificed, not Isaac?

(E) Learn about faith from Abraham.

- You will need scratch paper and writing utensils for use by class members. You might also want to have a large writing surface, such as a white board, chalkboard, or newsprint, with the appropriate markers for your use.
- Invite class members individually or within small groups to work on developing a "word picture" of faith. A "word picture" is a group of words or short phrases that help depict what that word means.
- Persons who are so inclined might wish to arrange their "word picture" into an appropriate shape.
- Allow time for persons to share their word pictures.
- Discuss:
—Given your word pictures of the concept of "faith," how would you go about defining faith?
—How has the example of Abraham added to your understanding of faith?
—What do you recognize as faith within your own life?

(F) Consider God's character.

We often say that the Bible is the book where more than anywhere else we learn what God is like. As we read passages like Genesis 22:1-19, it is appropriate and important that we pause to consider what such passages tell us about the nature of God.
- If class members have not already done so, make sure they take the time to read or review Genesis 22:1-19.
- Ask small groups or the class members as a whole to share the qualities of God they see present in this story.
- Discuss:
—Are the qualities you find present in God in this story ones you have expected God to have?
—What qualities that you would expect to find in God are missing from God as portrayed in this story?
—Does your perception of the character of God shift from one moment to the next as you read this story?
—Is the God portrayed in this Bible passage one whom you feel ready to worship?

Dimension 3:
What Does the Bible Mean to Us?

(G) Prepare to have your own faith tried.

- Read or summarize the material presented in the section entitled, "Trials of Faith" and in the sidebar "Praying the Lord's Prayer as Serious Business," pages 73–75 in the study book.
- The key to understanding the almost-sacrifice of Isaac appears to be that, through it, God sought to test the faithfulness of Abraham.
- Make sure class members understand that as we talk about "trials of faith" or "having one's faith tried" within the context of this chapter, we mean occasions when God intentionally seeks to find out how strong an individual's faith is. Sometimes, however, individuals will refer to their faith being tried when they actually mean that they feel frustrated by some occurrence.
- In small groups or within the class as a whole, discuss:
—What is the substance of faith? In other words, how would you go about defining or describing "faith"? How do you know "faith" when you see it? What are its defining characteristics?
—Did Abraham have faith as you have just defined it? In what ways and to what extent?
—How do you understand a "test" or "trial" of faith?
—What was the nature of the test through which God put Abraham and his faith?
—When was the last time God tried or tested *your* faith?
—What made that incident a test of your faith?
—How do you believe you fared in that test of faith?
—What do trials of faith peculiarly look like during our time?
—Are there any practical pieces of wisdom that you would suggest to someone who is undergoing a trial of faith?
—What biblical resources can you think of with which to help someone who is undergoing a trial of faith?
—If you were to be tried in a court of law on the charge of having faith in God, what sort of evidence might there be to convict you?

(H) Ponder the incomprehensibility of God.

- Read or summarize the information contained in the section, "An Incomprehensible Side to God," page 75 in the study book.
- Discuss:
—To what extent do you think you know God?

SACRIFICE

—What do you think you are supposed to know about God?
—Have you ever experienced an aspect or side to God that surprised or mystified you?
—To what extent do you think God has a "shadow" side that is not plainly evident to you and causes you to wonder just what God is like?
—What other Bible passages and stories can you think of that point to God as not being completely comprehensible by human beings?
—Do you think God wants to be completely knowable by and known to human beings?
—If there were one "mystery" about God you could have solved for the asking, what would it be?
—What steps can you take to try to know God better?

(I) Consider the concept of sacrifice.

- You may wish to consider using this learning segment especially if you previously used segment "C" in which class members research the Jewish practice of sacrifice. If you do not use segment "C," be sure to spend some time during class summarizing the information in this chapter's "Additional Bible Helps."
- Divide the class into groups of three to five persons.
- Ask each group to discuss:
  —What are some ways in which the word *sacrifice* is ordinarily used today?
  —How do the offerings many Christians present during worship services and at other times compare with the Jewish concept of sacrifice?
  —What, if anything, comes closest to being a modern equivalent to the Jewish concept of sacrifice?
  —What place does a notion of sacrifice have within your life? within the life of your class? within the life of your congregation?

Additional Bible Helps

The Jewish Sacrificial System

(Excerpts from *The Religious World of Jesus: An Introduction to Second Temple Palestinian Judaism*, by Frederick J. Murphy, pages 82–87. Copyright © 1991 by Abingdon Press. Used by permission.)

Sacrifice as Gift
The word "sacrifice" comes from the Latin *facere*, "to make," and *sacer*, "holy" or "sacred." To sacrifice something was to make it holy, to give it to God. It was to transfer it from the realm of the profane into the category of things that belong to God, the sacred. A ritual had to be performed to make the transfer, and that ritual was the sacrifice that God prescribed. A sacrifice would be useless if God were not there to receive it. For this reason, sacrifices were performed in the Temple. The Temple symbolized the three realms: the divine, the human, and the place of interaction between the two. There was a court before the Temple where Israel could assemble; God lived or appeared in the Holy of Holies; and the space between (the altar and the Holy Place) was a place of interaction where the priests gave God his animal sacrifices, grain, and incense.

. . . . .

Sacrifice as Food
If sacrifice meant giving something to God, and if that something was usually food, then the question arises whether Israel thought God actually needed to be fed. The conception of sacrifice as food lies behind Leviticus 3:11: "Then the priest shall turn these into smoke on the altar as a food offering by fire to the LORD." Such a conception was probably the origin of the phrase "sweet-smelling" as applied to sacrifices. Nonetheless, the Hebrew Bible seldom speaks of sacrifices as food. A protest against a more literal understanding of sacrifice as food appears in Psalm 50:12-13: "If I were hungry, I would not tell you; for the world and all that is in it is mine. Do I eat the flesh of bulls, or drink the blood of goats?" The psalm may be protesting a popular understanding of sacrifice. But the idea of feeding God is rare in the Hebrew Bible. Similarly there is little or no evidence for seeing the sacrificial feasts as attempts at mystical union with God or endeavors to assimilate the life force of the animal.

Blood
The Hebrew Bible gives two main reasons for sacrifice—gift (in petition or thanksgiving) and purification (expiation). In both cases the efficacy of sacrifice may have come from the nature of the blood shed.

. . . . .

The offering that was entirely burned on the altar was relatively rare. Usually the blood was poured out at the foot of the altar, and so the life of the animal was returned to God. Parts of the animal were burned on the altar, some (all of the rest, if it was a sin offering) was eaten by the priests as their portion, and some (if it was a peace offering) was eaten by those who brought the sacrifice. God always got the blood. The symbolism seems to be that the life of the animal belonged only to God. Humans were strictly forbidden to consume the blood, because then they would be consuming something belonging to God. This recalls Genesis. Before the flood, humans were vegetarians (Gen 1:29). After the flood, God gave permission to eat animals, provided that the blood was not eaten (Gen 9:2-5). This is one of the principles behind dietary laws (kosher laws) still followed by many Jews. To be kosher an animal must be killed in a way that ensures that there is no blood in the meat.

Atonement

The word translated "atone" or "expiate" in most texts is the Hebrew word *kipper*. In those contexts it means "to wipe off" or "to purge." Its object was not usually a person but a thing—the sanctuary, for example. This is clear in the case of the *hatta't*, usually translated "sin offering." It was not a gift to appease an angry God but a means of purging (cleansing) the sanctuary. A better translation for *hatta't* than "sin offering" would be "purification offering." The root idea is that sin defiled the sanctuary. The sanctuary was like a magnet that attracted the "dirt" caused by the sins of the people. The degree of seriousness of the sin determined the extent to which the defilement penetrated the sanctuary. The sanctuary could be purged of lesser sins by "washing off" the outer altar with the blood of the sin offering. Once a year the high priests entered the Holy of Holies to clean it of the defilement caused by sins. That occurred on the Day of Atonement, *Yom Kippur*, the holiest day of the Jewish year. It was necessary to purge God's dwelling of the defilement caused by the sin of the people because eventually the buildup of defilement would make it impossible for God to remain there. Purification made it possible for God to remain among the people, and God's presence among the people was necessary for the covenant to remain in effect. Thus, an important priestly function was maintenance of the covenant.

10

Esau and Jacob

Genesis 25:19-34; 27:1-45

LEARNING MENU
Keeping in mind the ways in which your class members learn best as well as their needs and interests, choose at least one learning segment from each of the three Dimensions.

Dimension 1: What Does the Bible Say?

(A) Discuss Dimension 1 questions.

- If many class members have not yet read the assigned Bible text and prepared answers to the Dimension 1 questions, allow time for them to work on them briefly at the beginning of the class session. Just be sure to reserve plenty of time to work on learning within Dimensions 2 and 3.
- Discussion of Dimension 1 questions may lead in these directions:
    1. The birthright is the eldest son's proper inheritance, both of his father's wealth as well as of the position as head of the household or clan. Although all sons would have been included in sharing in the estate of their father, the eldest son would have been entitled to an extra portion. This extra share is his simply by right of being born first.

    The blessing, on the other hand, has nothing to do with inheritance or birth order. In a blessing, one person "invokes" or calls forth good things upon another person. Within biblical contexts, the act of pronouncing a blessing—or a curse—often seemed to make the pronouncement so. Blessings are key in the Old Testament in that they often foreshadow the destiny of an individual or his or her descendants. Thus the blessing Isaac pronounced upon Jacob—even though Isaac intended it for Esau—foreshadowed the destiny Jacob would have at the expense of Esau.

    2. The short answer is that Jacob gained Esau's birthright by purchasing it for a bowl of stew once when Esau came in famished from working outdoors. Not far below the surface in the telling of this story are indications that on the one hand Esau did not think enough of his birthright to protect it carefully while Jacob took advantage of a bargain Esau might not have entered into seriously. However, the Israelite teller of this story says nothing about Jacob taking advantage of Esau, noting only that "thus Esau despised his birthright."

    3. Jacob obtained the blessing Isaac had intended for Esau by outright chicanery. With the help of their mother, Rebekah, Jacob masqueraded as Esau for the benefit of an ailing, blind Isaac. In fact, in Genesis 27:24 Jacob explicitly lied to his father, stating that

he was Esau. Therefore, it is no exaggeration to claim that Jacob lied, cheated, and stole in order to obtain the blessing intended for Esau.

4. For whatever reason, Rebekah favored her younger son, Jacob, at the expense of her elder son, Esau. She was the mastermind behind the plot for Jacob to steal Esau's blessing. She was quite willing to be a partner in deceiving her husband, Isaac, if it meant gaining an advantage for her beloved favorite son, Jacob. Rebekah's role seems overall to be that of a behind-the-scenes manipulator of people and events.

(B) Avoid the example of an "unmodel" family.

Not every person or family encountered in the Bible provides a positive example helpful for learning how to live good, Christian lives. Even the family of such key figures as the patriarchs and matriarch Isaac, Rebekah, Jacob, and Esau does not necessarily show us the right way to live. Even though the narrator of the Jacob stories never condemns his trickster behavior, we know that his scheming, lying, and cheating are simply not right. We know from criteria we gain elsewhere in the Bible that Jacob does not serve us as a good example of moral behavior.

- Divide the class into groups. Ask the groups to read the two passages assigned for this session: Genesis 25:19-34 and 27:1-45. The groups should then develop a list of all the behaviors present in the family system of Isaac, Rebekah, Esau, and Jacob that they would *not* recommend as enhancing healthy family behaviors and relationships.
- Next ask the groups to use their imaginations and devise a description of how Isaac, Rebekah, Esau, and Jacob should have behaved and related to one another in order to be considered a "model" worthy of imitation by Christians.
- Allow time for groups to share and discuss their findings.
- Discuss:
—How did you arrive at your lists of which family behaviors and relationships were unhealthy and which were those of a "model" family?
—Why do you think Isaac and Rebekah's family system turned out to be so dysfunctional—that is, unhealthy?
—What do you think the Israelites who first heard and read these stories about Esau and Jacob might have thought and felt about being descended from such a troubled family?
—What do you think a modern version of Isaac and Rebekah's family might look like?

Dimension 2:
What Does the Bible Mean?

(C) Research the theme of barrenness.

- You will need a variety of Bible dictionaries, commentaries, and concordances for class members to use during this learning segment. If your church has a library, you might want to consider holding this part of class there.
- Ask class members to read the story of the conception and the birth of the twins, Esau and Jacob: Genesis 25:19-26. Note that for a period of time Rebekah was considered barren. Remind class members that for many years Sarah had been barren as well.
- Ask class members individually or within small groups to research the theme of barrenness in the Bible. Encourage persons to try using the various Bible reference books you have provided for their use. For example, persons might look up the words *barren* and *barrenness* in a concordance to discover where else those words appear. They can then look up those citations in order to gain some understanding of their context and of how the words *barren* and *barrenness* are used there.
- As persons research the theme of barrenness, they might explore the following questions:
—Which other women in the Bible are described as being barren?
—Why did those women seem to be barren?
—What were their responses to their barrenness?
—Which of those women finally became pregnant, under what circumstances, and to whom did they give birth?
—In other locations in the Bible, how are words related to barrenness used? What kind of imagery is evoked for what purposes?
- Provide time for persons or groups to share and discuss their findings.

(D) Compare the differences between Esau and Jacob.

- You will need a large writing surface, such as newsprint, a white board, or a chalkboard, along with the appropriate marker.
- Divide the class into two groups (or an even number of groups if your class is large).
- Assign one group (or half of the groups) the task of listing everything they can learn on the basis of Genesis 25:19-34 and 27:1-45 about the lifestyle and personality of Esau. Assign the other group (or other half of the groups) the task of listing everything they can learn on the basis of those same Bible passages about the lifestyle and personality of Jacob.

- After a suitable period of time, call the whole class back together, Draw a line dividing your large writing surface in half vertically. Write as headings: *ESAU* and *JACOB*.
- As groups alternate, list characteristics of Esau and Jacob on the writing surface. As much as possible, try to write listed characteristics in such a way that Esau's and Jacob's traits balance each other. For example, if one of Esau's lifestyle characteristics is that he is a skillful hunter, you might list opposite of that characteristic Jacob's lifestyle trait of being a good cook.
- Discuss:
—What does this chart comparing traits of Esau and Jacob tell you?
—How do you think the differences between Esau and Jacob came to be?
—What can you tell about the way their differences caused Esau and Jacob to relate to each other?
—Which brother would you have preferred knowing? Why?
—Which brother do you think made the better candidate to be the bearer of the covenant promise? Why?

(E) Debate the better brother.

- You will probably not want to have the class do this learning segment if they have already done segment "D" above. Both learning segments cover much the same material and concerns, although with different slants.
- Divide the class into two groups.
- Assign each group one of the brothers: Esau or Jacob.
- Each group is to build as many good arguments as they can why its brother is the one more deserving to be the bearer of the covenant promise and why the other brother should not be entrusted with that responsibility.
- Allow each group three minutes to offer its best arguments as to why its brother is the one more deserving to be the bearer of the covenant promise.
- Next allow each group two minutes to rebut the arguments of the other group.
- Finally allow each group two minutes to offer its summary statements.
- After the debate is over, discuss:
—Which arguments did you really find more persuasive?
—If it had been up to you, which brother would you have chosen to be the bearer of the covenant promise?
—What qualities do you think should have determined which brother became the bearer of the covenant promise?
—Why do you think God chose Jacob to bear the covenant promise?

Dimension 3: What Does the Bible Mean to Us?

(F) Come to grips with God's scandals.

- Read or summarize the material contained in the section, "God Sometimes Scandalizes," pages 83–84 in the study book.
- The key biblical questions to discuss in this segment are
—If Jacob was a liar, cheat, and thief, then why did God choose Jacob to bear the promise of the covenant?
—Esau appears from our perspective to have been the wronged party; why did God not choose to side with Esau?
- Persons who want to research the "scandalous" persons listed in the section "God Sometimes Scandalizes" may wish to look up the following Bible passages:
  —Moses, the murderer: Exodus 2:11-15;
  —Rahab, the prostitute: Joshua 2:1-24;
  —Samson, the uncouth, muscle-bound warrior: Judges 15;
  —David, the traitor and adulterer: 1 Samuel 27 and 2 Samuel 11.
- Discuss the questions listed in the study book:
—In what ways does God scandalize you today?
—In what ways might God choose to use you in spite of the scandals of *your* life?

(G) Tell the story from Esau's perspective.

- You will need to provide scratch paper and writing utensils for use by the class members.
  The story of Esau and Jacob is told from the point of view of Jacob's descendants, the people of Israel. (In fact, keep in mind that as we shall learn in the next chapter, Jacob's name was changed to *Israel*. Jacob in many ways is the ideal Israelite.) In the telling of the story in the Bible, Jacob never seems to be criticized in spite of his lying, cheating, and stealing. If anyone looks bad in the passages covered in this session, it is Esau. But as many persons have observed, the victors get to write the history books. Jacob was the victor as far as the covenant was concerned. His descendants wrote the official history of Israel.
- Ask class members individually or as members of teams to read again Genesis 25:19-34 and 27:1-45.
- Individuals or groups should next work to rewrite these Bible passages from the perspective of Esau. As they work on these history revisions, they should keep in mind at least the following issues:
—What does Esau think of Jacob?
—Did Esau really despise his birthright?

—What really went on in the kitchen that day when Esau came in hungry and wanting to eat but Jacob ended up with Esau's birthright?
—Was Esau really as stupid as he seemed at times?
—What did Esau think of his parents, Isaac and Rebekah?
—What were Esau's feelings on the day when Jacob stole the blessing from Isaac that was intended for Esau?
—What were Esau's feelings when he heard the rather weak blessing Isaac still had available to offer to him?
—Do you think Esau was really capable of killing Jacob in revenge?
—Was Esau a victim?
• After revised histories have been written, ask persons or groups to share their efforts and to discuss them.
• Among the issues your class might discuss are:
—Was Esau treated fairly by God?
—Was Esau slighted by God for the sake of furthering the covenant with Abraham's descendants?
—Would you consider Esau to be a tragic figure?
—Would you be willing to be slighted to the extent that Esau was for the sake of furthering the kingdom of God?
• As an additional way of getting at the issues involved in accepting being slighted for the sake of building God's kingdom, try asking class members to read Philippians 4:2-3. This brief passage asks the leaders of the Christian church in Philippi to help two women mentioned by name—Euodia and Syntyche—to work together for the sake of the church. One may well imagine that Euodia and Syntyche might have thought that there was not enough room in the Philippian church for the both of them. But Paul urges them to "be of the same mind in the Lord." They should each set aside their need to be recognized for their work and focus on the effects of their work for furthering the gospel of Jesus Christ.

Additional Bible Helps

A Comparison of Esau and Jacob

This chart is offered as a quick reference tool to summarize information about Esau and Jacob as well as to provide a model for classes working on learning segment "D" above.

The Bible's Commentary on Esau

One source we have for trying to understand a biblical passage is the Bible itself. Although the Bible is not the only source we should go to as we seek understanding, it is a significant source we dare not neglect.

One of the most effective ways to discover what the Bible itself has to say by way of commentary on an event is to look up related names and terms in a Bible concordance. If you are using an unabridged concordance, every usage of the term you are looking up will be noted. A concise concordance, on the other hand, only lists those citations that its editor believes are the most relevant or significant.

One of the biggest puzzles a Bible student has in studying Genesis 25:19-34 and 27:1-45 is in trying to figure out why God should choose to favor Jacob over Esau. Turning to a concordance and looking up other references throughout the Bible to Esau can give us some clues as to what subsequent writers of Bible books thought of this person.

Perhaps the most telling comment on Esau comes already in Genesis 25, within the story of the selling of his birthright. The writer of the story, who of course is an Israelite and has some vested interest in preserving Jacob's reputation, notes in verse 34, "Thus Esau despised his birthright."

This appears to be the "official" Israelite position on why God chose Jacob over Esau. Esau had a moral flaw. He did not value his birthright properly. Although Jacob may have been guilty of coveting Esau's birthright (note in verse 31 how Jacob quickly takes the opportunity to ask Esau for his birthright), Esau apparently took his birthright for granted, or worse. Instead, Esau was more concerned about satisfying a short-term hunger and seemed to care less about his birthright, which could have long-term implications for him. One gets a sense from this passage that had Esau had a different moral character, his descendants might have well received the covenant with its special relation to God rather than Jacob's.

Most of the Bible's other references to Esau refer to him as representing his descendants, the Edomites who lived in Seir. For example, in passages in Jeremiah 49, in Obadiah, and in Malachi, words of God's judgment are pronounced upon Esau, who personifies the nation of Edom.

ESAU							
born first	name means "hairy"	hairy	"a skillful hunter"	"a man of the field"	loved by Isaac (because he was fond of game)	"despised his birthright"	impulsive
JACOB							
born gripping Esau's heel	name means "He supplants"	"a man of smooth skin"	"a quiet man"	"living in tents"	loved by Rebekah	bought Esau's birthright from him for some stew	scheming

Deuteronomy 2 implies that even though he was not the bearer of the covenant promise, Esau still had a special place in God's heart. As the Israelites pass through Seir on their way to the Promised Land, God warns them not to fight with Esau's descendants, for God has given them that land and they are still to be considered kin.

The most negative comment on Esau comes much later, in the Christian Letter to the Hebrews. Esau is not mentioned among the heroes of faith listed in Hebrews 11. However, as Hebrews 12 discusses some of the qualities of Christian living, the example of Esau is presented as one to avoid: "Puruse peace with everyone, and the holiness without which no one will see the Lord. See to it that no one fails to obtain the grace of God; that no root of bitterness springs up and causes trouble, and through it many become defiled. See to it that no one becomes like Esau, an immoral and godless person, who sold his birthright for a single meal. You know that later, when he wanted to inherit the blessing, he was rejected, for he found no chance to repent, even though he sought the blessing with tears" (Hebrews 12:14-17).

Jacob and God

Genesis 28:10-22; 32:3–33:20

LEARNING MENU

Keeping in mind the ways in which your class members learn best as well as their needs and interests, choose at least one learning segment from each of the three Dimensions.

Dimension 1: What Does the Bible Say?

(A) Discuss Dimension 1 questions.

- If many class members have not yet taken the time to read the assigned Bible texts and to work on the Dimension 1 questions, provide a limited amount of time for them to do so during class. The Bible texts for this session are Genesis 28:10-22 and 32:3–33:20.
- Discussion of Dimension 1 questions might lead in these directions:
  1. In one sense, Jacob did not "see" a stairway going up into heaven. According to Genesis 28:12 he "dreamed" about the ladder. He was asleep at the time. In another sense, Jacob "saw" the stairway in his dream because God wanted him to see it. The point of the dream of the stairway seems to be that the same God who was with Abraham and Isaac would also be with Jacob, even as Jacob ran away from his father's home in order to escape the wrath of Esau. In the dream, God confirms again the covenant that God had established with Abraham.
  2. Jacob immediately responded to his vision of God at Bethel with an attitude of worship. His first awareness upon awakening was that God was in that place in a special way even though Jacob had been unaware of God's presence as he had prepared for bed the night before. The awareness of God's presence brought forth feelings of fear and awe within Jacob. He had a sense that he was at a place where God's heavenly realm and earth intersected.

     To commemorate this encounter with God, Jacob set up a stone pillar and anointed it with oil. The ritual pouring of oil over an object (or person) indicated that it was set apart for God as sacred or holy. Centuries later, an Israelite sanctuary was built on what was thought to be the site of Jacob's pillar in the town of Bethel, which literally means "house of God."

     Jacob also made a vow to God, although the vow was somewhat weakened by the conditions that Jacob set upon it. He promised to acknowledge the LORD as God *if* God would go with him, protect him, and provide him with nourishment until he could return

again to Isaac's home in Beer-sheba.
3. As Jacob approached the moment of his reunion with Esau, he attempted to deceive him again in several ways:
— Jacob divided his household into two traveling groups, with the intent that if Esau's army fell upon one group and destroyed it, the other group might escape.
— Jacob sent a large gift of livestock to Esau, intended as a peace offering, a bribe, or simply as an attempt to cause Esau to think more favorably of him.
— Jacob divided the large gift of livestock into smaller droves, leaving space between the droves, in an attempt to make Esau think the gift was even larger than it was.
— As Jacob came near enough to Esau to know that they would meet the next day, Jacob sent his household and property across the Jabbok River, remaining alone—and safer—on the far shore.
— Even after they were reunited and at least somewhat reconciled, Jacob lied to Esau about joining him in Esau's homeland of Seir. Instead, as soon as he could, Jacob traveled west away from Esau, who was headed south.
4. The outcome of Jacob's wrestling match as such appears to be a draw. The text in Genesis 32:24-31 states that the stranger was not winning against Jacob. Verse 25 implies that the stranger may even have cheated (against the cheater!) by striking Jacob in such a way that his hip joint was severely injured. Even then, Jacob refused to let the stranger go until the stranger blessed him.

The greater outcome of the wrestling match was Jacob's realization that he had struggled face to face with God. God blessed Jacob at the close of their wrestling match, and renamed Jacob "Israel." *Israel* literally means "The one who strives with God" or "God strives." By this new name would Jacob's descendants be known—Israel.

(B) Trace Jacob's journeys.

- Ask class members to work individually or within small groups.
- Invite class members to skim through the material in Genesis 28:10–33:20, noting places through which Jacob traveled or where he stayed.
- Using the map on page 87 of the study book, persons should mark the places Jacob stayed in or moved through and trace a possible route on which Jacob traveled on his journeys.
- If you want class members to do a more in-depth map study, provide Bible atlases, Bible dictionaries, and commentaries for their use; or arrange for the class to use the church library, if there is one. Ask class members to use those Bible reference tools to look up the various places mentioned in the Bible text. Ask them to investigate and discuss:

— Through what kind of terrain did Jacob move?
— How far did Jacob travel during his twenty-year journey?
— At what kinds of places did Jacob encounter God in special ways?
— What do the place names mean? Which places did Jacob name?
— Based on your research, what mental images do you have of
  — Beer-sheba, where Isaac lived;
  — Bethel, where Jacob dreamed about a stairway going up into heaven;
  — Paddan-aram, where Jacob worked for Laban and married Leah and Rachel;
  — Peniel, where Jacob wrestled through the night with a man;
  — the place near the Jabbok River where Jacob was reunited with Esau.

Dimension 2:
What Does the Bible Mean?

(C) Encounter the faces of God.

- Divide the class into three groups.
- Assign one of these Bible passages to each of the groups:
  — Genesis 28:10-22
  — Genesis 32:22-32
  — Genesis 33:1-17

In each of these three passages, Jacob encountered a "face" of God:
— as God appeared to Jacob in the dream of the stairway going up into heaven;
— as God wrestled with Jacob;
— as Jacob realized that to experience Esau's gracious reconciliation was "like seeing the face of God."

- Ask each group to read its Bible passage and to discuss the following:
— In what way did Jacob see "the face of God"?
— What qualities of God did Jacob experience in this encounter?
— What qualities of his own character did Jacob show as he encountered this "face of God"?
— How did Jacob respond to encountering this "face of God"?
- Allow time for groups to share and discuss their findings.

(D) Sing, "We Are Climbing Jacob's Ladder."

"We Are Climbing Jacob's Ladder" is an African-American spiritual based on Genesis 28:10-17. Almost every Christian will have learned and sung this song at some time in his or her life, whether in Sunday school or at a church camp or during a worship service.

- If your class enjoys singing together, they may wish to sing it as one of their learning activities for this session.
- You, or someone you have recruited to lead the singing, may line out the verses instead of relying upon a printed hymnal.

"We Are Climbing Jacob's Ladder"

1. We are climbing Jacob's ladder,
   We are climbing Jacob's ladder,
   We are climbing Jacob's ladder;
   Soldiers of the cross.

2. Every round goes higher, higher...

3. Sinner, do you love my Jesus...

4. If you love him, why not serve him?...

5. We are climbing higher, higher...

- After singing this spiritual, you may want to discuss these questions as a whole class:
—What seems to be the primary message of "We Are Climbing Jacob's Ladder"?
—In what ways is the song based upon the Bible text?
—In what ways does the song move beyond the Bible text?
—When was the first time you recall singing "We Are Climbing Jacob's Ladder"? What was the occasion? Where were you? What was its meaning for you then?

(E) Look for the difference twenty years makes.

- Ask class members to review all the material they have read so far about Jacob, extending from Genesis 25:19 through 33:20.
- Note that the material in Genesis 29:1–32:2 spans a twenty-year period between the time when Jacob runs away from Esau's revenge and the time when Jacob returns to face Esau.
- Ask persons individually or as members of small groups to consider what changes, if any, there have been in Jacob's personality, character, and life situation during that twenty-year period.

- Discuss as a class:
—What differences do twenty years make in the life of Jacob?
—How has Jacob's personality and character changed, if at all, during that time?
—How has Esau's personality and character appeared to change, if at all, during the twenty years Jacob has been gone?
—Using your imagination, what do you think might have happened had Jacob remained in Beer-sheba with Esau, Isaac, and Rebekah, instead of running off to Paddan-aram?

Dimension 3: What Does the Bible Mean to Us?

(F) Consider the ways you encounter God.

In the Bible texts for this session, Jacob encounters God in several different ways:
—in a dream (Genesis 28:10-17);
—in a vision of angels (Genesis 32:1-2);
—in a long night's wrestling match (Genesis 32:22-32);
—in the face of his estranged brother, Esau (Genesis 33:10).

- In pairs, ask your class members to discuss the following questions:
—Do the ways in which Jacob encounters God affect his experience of who God is?
—In what ways have you encountered God? Have you, like Jacob, encountered God
  —in a dream?
  —in a vision?
  —in a long night's wrestling match?
  —in the face of another person, perhaps someone from whom you had been alienated for some reason?
—In what other ways have you encountered God?
—What has God been like in those encounters?
—After Jacob encountered God in the wrestling match at Peniel, Jacob left limping from being injured in the hip. Do your encounters with God ever leave you limping from an injury? If so, in what ways?

(G) Recall the awe felt in the presence of God.

When Jacob experienced his dream of the stairway into heaven, upon awakening he felt some rather strong emotions that are reported in the biblical text: "And he was afraid, and said, 'How awesome is this place!'" (Genesis 28:16-17).

- Ask persons to talk together in pairs, discussing these questions:

—How would you describe a feeling of awe?
—Have you ever had an experience in which you felt the presence of God? What did you feel in that experience?
—The Bible reports Jacob feeling fear when he awoke from his dream in which he encountered God. To what extent do you associate a feeling of fear with a sense of the presence of God?
—What would it take for you to feel the presence of God?
—Have you ever felt awe in the presence of God during a worship service? What do you think it would take for you to feel awe in the presence of God during a worship service?
—Have you ever felt awe in the presence of God during the personal practice of prayer or other spiritual discipline? What was it like? What do you think it would take for you to feel awe in the presence of God during your personal spiritual life?
—To what extent do you think it is necessary to feel awe and/or fear of God to say that you have had a "religious" experience?
—What other feelings besides awe or fear might a person experience in the presence of God?

Additional Bible Helps

"Come, O Thou Traveler Unknown"
The hymn, "Come, O Thou Traveler Unknown," was written by Methodist leader and English hymn writer Charles Wesley in 1742, based on the Bible text Genesis 32:24-32. English poet Isaac Watts considered it one of the best poems of the day. It is offered here as one eighteenth-century commentary on this passage, showing how one part of historic Christian tradition understood the meaning of the text.

One good way to learn how Christians of previous generations have understood various Bible texts is to examine how they have turned them into hymns. You might try looking in the back of your church's hymnal to see if there is an index showing which hymns are based on which Bible texts.

Come, O Thou Traveler Unknown
Come, O thou Traveler unknown,
whom still I hold, but cannot see!
My company before is gone,
and I am left alone with thee;
with thee all night I mean to stay
and wrestle till the break of day.

I need not tell thee who I am,
my misery and sin declare;
thyself hast called me by my name,
look on thy hands and read it there.
But who, I ask thee, who art thou?
Tell me thy name, and tell me now.

In vain thou strugglest to get free.
I never will unloose my hold;
art thou the man that died for me?
The secret of thy love unfold;
wrestling, I will not let thee go
till I thy name, thy nature know.

Wilt thou not yet to me reveal
thy new, unutterable name?
Tell me, I still beseech thee, tell,
to know it now resolved I am;
wrestling, I will not let thee go,
till I thy name, thy nature know.

'Tis all in vain to hold thy tongue
or touch the hollow of my thigh;
though every sinew be unstrung,
out of my arms thou shalt not fly;
wrestling I will not let thee go
till I thy name, thy nature know.

What though my shrinking flesh complain
and murmur to contend so long?
I rise superior to my pain:
when I am weak then I am strong,
and when my all of strength shall fail
I shall with the God-man prevail.

My strength is gone, my nature dies,
I sink beneath thy weighty hand,
faint to revive, and fall to rise;
I fall, and yet by faith I stand;
I stand and will not let thee go
till I thy name, thy nature know.

Yield to me now—for I am weak
but confident in self-despair!
Speak to my heart, in blessing speak,
be conquered by my instant prayer:
speak, or thou never hence shalt move,
and tell me if thy name is Love.

'Tis Love! 'tis Love! thou diedst for me,
I hear thy whisper in my heart.
The morning breaks, the shadows flee,
pure Universal Love thou art:
to me, to all, thy mercies move—
thy nature, and thy name is Love.

My prayer hath power with God; the grace
unspeakable I now receive;
through faith I see thee face to face,
I see thee face to face, and live!
In vain I have not wept and strove—
thy nature, and thy name is Love.

I know thee, Savior, who thou art,
Jesus, the feeble sinner's friend;
nor wilt thou with the night depart,
but stay and love me to the end:
thy mercies never shall remove,
thy nature, and thy name is Love.

The Sun of Righteousness on me
hath risen with healing in his wings:
withered my nature's strength; from thee
my soul its life and succor brings;
my help is all laid up above;
thy nature, and thy name is Love.

Contented now upon my thigh
I halt, till life's short journey end;
all helplessness, all weakness I
on thee alone for strength depend;
nor have I power from thee to move:
thy nature, and thy name is Love.

Lame as I am, I take the prey,
hell, earth, and sin with ease overcome;
I leap for joy, pursue my way,
and as a bounding hart fly home,
through all eternity to prove
thy nature, and thy name is Love.

LEARNING MENU
Keeping in mind the ways in which your class members learn best as well as their needs and interests, choose at least one learning segment from each of the three Dimensions.

Dimension 1: What Does the Bible Say?

(A) Discuss Dimension 1 Questions.

- If many class members have not taken the time before class to read the Bible passages assigned for this session and to answer the Dimension 1 questions, provide a limited amount of time for them to do so at the start of the class session.
- Discussion of Dimension 1 questions might lead in these directions:
  1. Joseph's brothers resented him for at least five reasons:
     —Only he and his younger brother, Benjamin, were Jacob's sons by Rachel, Jacob's favorite wife. All the other brothers were born to Leah, Zilpah, or Bilhah. (See the chart, "Baby Wars," page 96 in the study book.)
     —He was their father Jacob's favorite son: "Now Israel [Jacob] loved Joseph more than any other of his children, because he was the son of his old age. . . . But when his brothers saw that their father loved him more than all his brothers, they hated him, and could not speak peaceably to him" (Genesis 37:3-4).
     —His father gave him a special coat—depending on the translation it either had many colors or very long sleeves. Either way, he would not have done any work while wearing the special coat. Yet when his father sent him out to see how his brothers were doing with the flock at Shechem, Joseph wore the special coat, both flaunting his favorite position before his brothers as well as making it plain that he was not about to do any work.
     —Joseph "tattled" on his brothers: "he was a helper to the sons of Bilhah and Zilpah, his father's wives; and Joseph brought a bad report of them to his father" (Genesis 37:2).
     —Joseph told his brothers about two dreams he had in which representations of his brothers bowed down to him in obeisance: "So they hated him even more because of his dreams and his words" (Genesis 37:8; see also verse 11).
  2. In these biblical texts, dreams foreshadow events that are to happen:
     —Joseph dreams in Genesis 37:5-11 of representa-

tions of his brothers bowing down to him. Years later, his brothers in fact bow down to him when, unknown to them, he has become Pharaoh's prime minister. In the immediate passage, however, these dreams serve as an occasion for Joseph's brothers to resent him yet more deeply.

—While in an Egyptian prison, Joseph interprets the dreams of two fellow inmates, forecasting that the chief cupbearer would be restored to Pharaoh's favor while the royal baker would be executed. Within the immediate context, Joseph's interpretation of these dreams will cause the chief cupbearer to remember him two years later when Pharaoh has dreams needing interpretation.

—Pharaoh's dreams of the seven sleek and fat cows and the seven ugly and thin cows, as well as of the seven plump and good ears of grain and the seven thin and blighted ears of grain foreshadow the seven years of plenty and the seven years of famine about to come upon Egypt. Within the immediate context, Joseph's interpretation of these dreams brings him to Pharaoh's attention when none of the wise people of Egypt are able to interpet the dreams. Pharaoh makes Joseph his prime minister, second only to Pharaoh in power within the entire Egyptian empire.

3. Both when Joseph interprets the dreams of the chief cupbearer and the royal baker and when he interprets the dreams of Pharaoh, he makes it very plain that he has nothing to do with interpreting the dreams—it is God who interprets dreams. We have no indication within the biblical text about how Joseph comes to be able to share God's interpretations of these dreams.

4. By the end of Genesis 41, Joseph holds a position roughly equivalent to prime minister. Joseph holds power second only to that of Pharaoh. By placing his signet ring on Joseph's hand, Pharaoh signifies that Joseph now speaks with Pharaoh's own authority.

(B) Decide what to do with Joseph.

- Tell the members of the class to imagine themselves to be Joseph's older half brothers. If you have ten class members or fewer, you might want to assign them names: Reuben, Simeon, Levi, Judah, Dan, Naphtali, Gad, Asher, Issachar, and Zebulun. (Benjamin was Joseph's younger, full brother and would not have been present.)
- Inform these "half brothers" that they are going to have to decide what to do with Joseph, their younger half brother whom they do not like at all. In fact, because he is their father's favorite son, because he is something of a tattletale, because he has pretensions of lording it over them, because he has come out here to Shechem with his fancy coat that their father had given only to him and he obviously has no intentions of doing any of the work of shepherding, they *hate* him. They are miles away from Jacob, off on their own watching the sheep graze on the pastureland, and Joseph walks into their hands. They can do what they want with Joseph.
- Read aloud Genesis 37:12-24.
- Tell the half brothers they have five minutes in which to decide what to do with Joseph.
- After the brothers have made their decision (or the time has expired without a decision), read aloud Genesis 37:25-36 to describe what the brothers actually decided to do with Joseph.

Dimension 2: What Does the Bible Mean?

(C) Research the Egyptian Empire.

- You will need to provide copies of Bible reference tools, such as Bible dictionaries, Bible atlases, and commentaries. If your church has a library, you might want the class to work on this learning segment there.
- Ask class members to work individually or within teams to discover everything they can in a given period of time (such as fifteen or twenty minutes) about the Egyptian Empire as it existed at the time of Joseph. They will want to concentrate on the period roughly around 1600 B.C., during the Fifteenth through Seventeenth Dynasties of Egypt, when the capital of the empire was at Thebes.
- After the time for research has expired, invite persons (or teams) to share and discuss their findings.
- Ask persons to imagine what it might have been like for Joseph, a boy abducted and sold into slavery away from his family abruptly at the age of seventeen, to arrive as a slave in the capital city of the Egyptian Empire.

(D) Focus on dreams.

- Divide the class into three groups.
- Assign each group one set of dreams:
—Joseph's dreams in Genesis 37:5-11;
—the prison dreams of the chief cupbearer and the royal baker in Genesis 40:1-23;
—Pharaoh's dreams in Genesis 41:1-45.
- Ask each group to consider the following questions concerning the dreams on which they are focusing:
—Who had the dreams?
—What was the substance of the actual dreams?
—Who interpreted the dreams?
—What were the interpretations of the dreams?
—What effect did the dreams and their interpretations have upon the dreamers and those around them?

—How did the dreams affect Joseph?
—In what ways did the dreams and their interpretations seem to further God's purposes?
- Read or summarize the information found in the section entitled, "Dreams," pages 99–100 in the study book.
- Discuss as a whole class the question that ends this section: What do you make of your dreams?

(E) Inquire into Joseph's character.

As indicated in the "Additional Bible Helps" for this chapter, Jewish tradition gave to Joseph the title of *Tzaddik*, which means "the Just One."
- Divide the class members into groups of five to seven persons.
- Inform the groups that they are about to serve as special "search" committees on behalf of Pharaoh. Pharaoh is looking for someone to fill the position of a most trusted advisor. He is intrigued at the prospect of hiring this Hebrew prisoner by the name of *Joseph* who had interpreted Pharaoh's dreams so admirably when no one else could. The search committees are to work their way through Genesis 37:1–41:49, looking for evidence that Joseph may or may not be a good person to hire for the position of a most trusted advisor to Pharaoh. Among other things, they should consider the following questions during their inquiry:
—What in Joseph's past actions give some indication to how he might act in the future?
—What evidence can you find regarding Joseph's character? For example, is he trustworthy? reliable? able to solve problems?
—What would past employers or supervisors have to say about Joseph?
—What recommendation would you make to Pharaoh concerning whether to hire Joseph? Why would you make that recommendation?

Dimension 3: What Does the Bible Mean to Us?

(F) Publish the leadership secrets of Joseph.

- You will need to provide scratch paper and writing utensils for use by class members.
- Read or summarize the information found in the section entitled, "Leadership and Power," pages 100–101 in the study book.
- Divide the class members into groups of three to five persons.
- Mention that during the 1990's, a number of business management books have been written and published that offer management and leadership ideas based on the writings or the actions of various historic leaders. For example, books of the so-called "leadership secrets" of Sitting Bull, Abraham Lincoln, and Attila the Hun have all shown up on bookstore shelves.
- Assign each group the task of skimming through the material found in Genesis 37:1–41:49. They are then to produce an outline for a new book on "The Leadership Secrets of Joseph."
- Ask groups to share their outlines with the whole class. Discussion might follow along these lines:
—How might Joseph have defined the word *leadership*?
—To what extent was Joseph a good or poor leader?
—How would you describe Joseph's leadership abilities?
—What "leadership secrets" that you found in your research on Joseph might you be able to apply in your life at home or in your business?

(G) Prepare for disaster.

- Ask the class members to read or review the material in Genesis 41. In this chapter, Joseph interprets Pharaoh's dreams about an impending severe famine coming upon Egypt. Joseph takes God's interpretation of Pharaoh's dreams a step beyond the mere announcement of the coming tragedy. Joseph also offers a four-point proposal for dealing with the famine:
  1. Pharaoh should appoint a wise, discerning leader to make decisions on Pharaoh's behalf in order to deal with the coming crisis.
  2. Pharaoh should also appoint a number of overseers (read "crisis management officials") who will collect ("seize") twenty percent of the food produced in Egypt during each of the seven plentiful years yet to come.
  3. This food, particularly the grain, should be placed in granaries in the cities of Egypt to be saved against the coming years of famine.
  4. This reserve of food will save Egyptians against starvation during the famine.

     Pharaoh chooses to appoint the thirty-year-old Joseph to be the leader who will make decisions in Pharaoh's name.
- As a whole class or in small groups of three to five persons, discuss:
—What do you like or dislike about Joseph's four-point proposal?
—Do you think God warns us about disasters today?
—If so, what kinds of disasters do you think God is warning us about today?
—In what ways might God warn us about disasters?
—How well do you think we would be able to hear God warning us about disasters?
—How well do you think our community's and nation's

leaders would be able to hear God warning us about disasters?
—What do you think Christians are called to do in the face of impending disasters?
—What do you think your church or your class might be doing now in order to prepare for a coming disaster of some sort?

Note that Joseph came into a position in which he not only was able to help himself as he moved into a position of prominence, he also was able to help his family as we shall hear in the next chapter. Less noticed but also significantly, Joseph was able to help innumerable Egyptians and others in the regions near Egypt.

• Discuss:
—To what extent should Christians help persons outside of their congregation or community who are suffering from disasters of various kinds?
—What are some disaster relief efforts in which your congregation or class is already involved?
—What additional efforts might your congregation or class make in the area of disaster relief?

Additional Bible Helps

Joseph the Righteous

The following excerpts are from *Messengers of God: Biblical Portraits and Legends*, by Elie Wiesel; Touchstone Books, 1985. Copyright © 1976 by Elirion Associates, Inc. Reprinted by permission of Simon & Schuster, Inc. Nobel Peace Prize winner Wiesel has woven together legends and stories from Scripture and from the Jewish *Midrash*. The *Midrash* is a collection of commentaries (midrashim) that were written down by rabbis in the period between A.D. 400 through 1200, in order to fill in gaps within the biblical record and to provide commentary on the Torah, the first five books of what Christians call the Old Testament.

> Talmudic imagination has turned [Joseph] into a sort of superstar. His very name is said to have caused the angels to tremble. We owe him the miraculous crossing of the Red Sea. But also, said an ancient sage, all the sufferings to be endured by Israel until the end of time are rooted in those inflicted on Joseph by his brothers.... Among the ancestors, no other had a right to his surname: *Tzaddik*. [*Tzaddik* means "the just."] Abraham was obedient, Isaac was brave, Jacob was faithful. Only Joseph was just.
>
> Just—he? He who married a woman who was not Jewish, a daughter of Egypt who brought up his children among pagans? He who led a life of luxury in the splendor of the royal palace? He who wielded quasi-absolute power and seemed to love it? What did he do to deserve this prestigious title?
>
> . . . . .
>
> In the Midrash the answer is simple: because Joseph was able to overcome his sexual urges. Despite the atmosphere of overt sensuality that prevailed in Egypt, he resisted adulterous wives, Potiphar's and others: Day after day Joseph saw a number of princesses and courtesans, some covered with jewels, others with perfume, still others . . . with nothing at all; and every one of them was seductive. But Joseph remained chaste.
>
> Another text offers this image: When Joseph went in and out of the royal palace, the princesses stood at their windows and threw him their jewels, earrings and bracelets, to attract his attention—but he never looked up. For our ancient sages, that evidently was reason enough to crown him *Tzaddik*.
>
> Not for me. I readily admit that a *Tzaddik* should be able to resist temptations, but I would prefer to see the concept enlarged to include temptations beyond those inherent in sexuality.
>
> First let us define the term *Tzaddik*. In Arabic it means friend. In Hebrew it is the opposite of *Rasha*, wicked. *Rasha* is he who sins against man, not necessarily against God. He who deserts his community is a *Rasha*. He who harms his friends is a *Rasha*. To betray one's comrades, to flout one's people, those are acts of a *Rasha*.
>
> Conversely, the term *Tzaddik* is defined by relationships between men, not necessarily between man and God. A *Tzaddik* is he who resists temptations, not necessarily tests. Tests imply God; temptations are human. Abraham, tested by God, was not a *Tzaddik*. Joseph was.
>
> Joseph had to overcome inner obstacles not in order to come closer to God, but to his fellow men. His own brothers. He had good reasons to repudiate them, to hate them, to drive them from his house and memory; for him they represented a source of grief and evil.
>
> He had equally good reasons to distrust women; the most beautiful and powerful among them caused him to be thrown into prison.
>
> He had every reason to distrust people in general.
>
> . . . . .
>
> Joseph knew—and who was in a better position to know—that to be the first Jewish prince in history, to be the first to liberate Jews outside their homeland, would be difficult and unrewarding. A descendant of [his older brother Judah's] was to wear the crown of

(From *Messengers of God: Biblical Portraits and Legends*. Copyright © 1976 by Elirion Associates, Inc. Reprinted by permission of Simon & Schuster, Inc.)

Jewish sovereignty, symbolizing eternal promise and eternal dawn.

And yet, Joseph did not despair.

He assumed his destiny and tried to give it meaning from within. He lived his eternal life in the here-and-now, demonstrating that it is possible for the slave to be prince, for the dreamer to link his past to the future, for the victor to open himself to the supreme passion that is love.

What a story: it tells us in one breath that the first exile was caused by the disruptive jealousy of men who were brothers; that exile leads to redemption if only one dreams of it without despair and . . . remains true to oneself.

Joseph was not born a *Tzaddik*, nor did he have the childhood or the education of a *Tzaddik*; that is why his triumph excites us. Whatever Joseph obtained for himself, he owed only to himself.

His reward? Moses personally took care of his funeral. Why such a privilege? Because while his ancestors had to deal with God and proved themselves worthy, Joseph had to deal with men and proved himself no less worthy. To suffer at the hands of God is less painful—or painful in a different way—than suffering the cruelty of men, even if they are our brothers, particularly if they are our brothers. Joseph, the first Jew to suffer at the hands of Jews, succeeded in mastering his grief and disappointment and linking his fate to theirs.

Joseph—a *Tzaddik?* The title was, unquestionably, deserved. In the Biblical text there is another adjective that describes him well: beautiful.

13

RESTORATION

Genesis 42–45

LEARNING MENU
Keeping in mind the ways in which your class members learn best as well as their needs and interests, choose at least one learning segment from each of the three Dimensions.

Dimension 1: What Does the Bible Say?

(A) Discuss Dimension 1 questions.

- If many class members have not taken the time to read the Bible texts assigned for this session and to work on the Dimension 1 questions, then set aside a limited amount of time at the beginning of the class session for them to do so.
- The Bible text for this session is lengthy: Genesis 42:1–45:28. One way to spend a minimal amount of time learning what took place in these chapters would be to divide the class into four groups. Assign each group one of the four chapters—chapters 42, 43, 44, and 45. Groups are to read through their chapter and prepare a summary to present to the rest of the class.
- Discussion of Dimension 1 questions might lead in these directions:

1. According to Genesis 42:6, "Joseph's brothers came and bowed themselves before him with their faces to the ground." In this way they fulfill the dream Joseph reported to them in Genesis 37:5-8, in which "There we were, binding sheaves in the field. Suddenly my sheaf rose and stood upright; then your sheaves gathered around it, and bowed down to my sheaf."

2. At first glance, Joseph's testing of his brothers may be difficult to understand except as a bit of revenge, however petulant. Yet Joseph may have had more in mind than a simple payback for past grievances. The primary reason for keeping Simeon as hostage may have been to make sure the brothers do return with Benjamin as they had promised. Moreover, it may have been an attempt to play on the brothers' sense of guilt: Just as they had once before told Jacob that a son of his was missing, now they again have to tell him that another son is being held a hostage far away in Egypt.

3. The tricks that Joseph plays by hiding money in the sacks of his brothers after they have left for home may serve in part the purpose of throwing them off balance. The money also turns the food the brothers had bought from the Egyptian government into gifts provided by the generosity of Joseph. It may be that Joseph wanted to provide his family with gifts with-

out them yet knowing who he was or that he was even still alive.

The trick of placing Joseph's divining cup into Benjamin's sack seems to have a more serious motive. Joseph's steward pronounced the sentence that should the cup be found in one of the brothers' sacks, that brother would become a slave in the prime minister's household. When the cup is found in Benjamin's sack, the remaining brothers are faced with a difficult decision: Will they permit another brother to remain a slave in Egypt—as they had permitted Joseph to go into slavery in Egypt years before—while they go free? Judah answers for the brothers: They will all remain as slaves; or if that is not acceptable, then at least he, Judah, will "remain as a slave to my lord in place of the boy; and let the boy go back with his brothers" (Genesis 44:33).

4. Besides the fulfillment Joseph may have found in his life from rising to the high position of prime minister of the most powerful empire in that part of the world, Joseph states to his brothers the real meaning he had found for his life: "God sent me before you to preserve for you a remnant on earth, and to keep alive for you many survivors. So it was not you who sent me here, but God; he has made me a father to Pharaoh, and lord of all his house and ruler over all the land of Egypt" (Genesis 45:7-8).

(B) Keep track of the brothers.

- You will want to provide copies of Bible dictionaries and concordances for class members to use.

   Even though Genesis 37:2 states, "This is the story of the family of Jacob," most of what follows tells about Joseph. The other brothers play seemingly minor parts in the story of Joseph and how he came into a position to save the family in the midst of a life-threatening famine and to bring the family into Egypt where four centuries later they will be liberated from slavery by God. Even though Reuben is the oldest of the brothers and even though through Judah's line King David will later be born, neither of those brothers play much of a role in the story of Joseph.

   One way, however, for your class to become more familiar with the Bible passage covered in this session, is to trace the activities of Joseph's brothers.

- Divide your class members into groups of three to five persons. Assign one or more brothers to each group: Reuben, Simeon, Levi, Judah, Dan, Naphtali, Gad, Asher, Issachar, Zebulon, and Benjamin. (Class members may also find a list of these brothers in the chart titled, "Baby Wars," page 96 in the study book.)

- Ask the groups to skim through the Bible passages covered in Chapter 12 and in this chapter, noting the occasions when the brother(s) assigned to them are mentioned. For further research, groups may want to look up the brother(s) assigned to them in a Bible dictionary and concordance to learn about that brother's significance.

- Allow time for groups to report and discuss their findings.

Dimension 2: What Does the Bible Mean?

(C) Rewrite the story from God's point of view.

- You will need to provide scratch paper and writing utensils for class members to use.

   In the story of Joseph, God is spoken of in the third person, as if God is distant from the action. This perspective is different from that encountered earlier in Genesis, where God spoke directly to the first humans, to Noah, to Abraham, and to Jacob.

- Ask class members, individually or in small groups, to rewrite the action found in Genesis 42:1–45:28 as if it were being told from God's point of view. They may want to key in on the verses where God is mentioned within the dialogue. They may also want to consider whether all the action described in these chapters is really relevant from God's point of view.

- Invite class members or groups to share their rewriting efforts.

- Discuss:

—In what ways does the story told in these four chapters become different when told from God's point of view than from the way that Genesis tells the story as if it were told from over Joseph's shoulder?

—How is God seen to be at work in the actions of these four chapters?

—In your rewritings of these chapters, what does God think about the actions and the speeches of the humans?

—What is the point of this story from God's point of view?

(D) Plan the reunion.

The story found in the four chapters of Genesis covered in this chapter move toward the restoration or reunion of Joseph with his brothers and his father. By the end of Genesis 45, Joseph has seen all of the brothers from whom he had been separated for so many years, Joseph has revealed himself to them, and Jacob has learned that Joseph, whom he had thought long dead, was still alive and ruling over Egypt at the side of Pharaoh. By the end of Genesis 45, all is right in Israel's world.

If anything, however, Joseph's reunion with his brothers strikes many modern readers as being somewhat bizarre. The tricks Joseph plays on his brothers seem almost pointless, as does Joseph's hiding of his identity. Only after keeping his brothers dangling on the line for three chapters and for probably well over a year does Joseph finally celebrate being together again with his brothers.

- Divide your class members into groups of three to five persons.
- Assign the task to each group of planning how Joseph might have done his reunion with his family differently. Encourage them to use their imaginations and creativity in considering how Joseph and his family should have done up their reunion right.
- Allow time for groups to report on and discuss their plans.
- Discuss:

—Why do you think Joseph carried out his reunion with his brothers in the manner described in Genesis?

—What do you think Joseph's feelings were as he saw and recognized his brothers again after all those years and the way they had treated him when they had last been together?

—How do you think Joseph's brothers felt when he finally revealed his identity to them in Chapter 45?

—Why do you think Joseph finally acted so charitably toward his half brothers?

Dimension 3: What Does the Bible Mean to Us?

(E) Roleplay Joseph tricking his brothers.

Many modern readers find it difficult to understand what was going on as Joseph placed first money and then his divining cup into his brothers' packs after they left him to return home to Jacob. They find it even more difficult to understand the meaning, if any, underlying that action. One way to work on understanding what was going on is to roleplay the various characters involved in these actions.

- If you have a large class, you might want to divide the class members into four groups. Each group is to study a different chapter assigned for this session (Genesis 42–45) and to develop a roleplay based on the action of that chapter. They are not to worry about using the precise words or actions presented in the Bible text of their chapter. Instead they are to get a sense of the dynamics of the chapter and to decide how they wish to play out that action. One person in each group should play the part of Joseph. The groups will have to decide which other parts are also necessary to fill.
- If you have a smaller class, rotate the role of Joseph among different class members for each chapter. Other class members may play other roles as needed. The class will have to work together on how the action of each chapter should play itself out.
- Roleplay the action of each chapter. Afterward discuss what class members learned by studying the Bible material in this way.
- Discuss:

—How did it feel to play the role of Joseph?

—How did it feel to play the roles of Joseph's half brothers?

—What do you think was really going on between Joseph and his brothers in the action of these chapters?

—What emotions do you think were being felt by the various persons whose roles were played? Were you getting in touch with any of those feelings as you played your role?

—To what extent do you think Joseph had planned for a long time what he would do if he ever encountered his half brothers again?

—If you had been Joseph, would you have put your half brothers through the tricks that Joseph did? What would you have done differently? What would you have done the same?

—If you had been Joseph's half brothers, how would you have reacted to the tricks Joseph had played on you, particularly once you learned who Joseph was?

(F) Consider what you believe about providence.

- You will need copies of Bible dictionaries and theological dictionaries for use by class members.

  The climax of the entire cycle of Joseph stories comes in Genesis 45:7-8: "God sent me before you to preserve for you a remnant on earth, and to keep alive for you many survivors. So it was not you who sent me here, but God; he has made me a father to Pharaoh, and lord of all his house and ruler over all the land of Egypt."

- Ask class members individually or in small groups to research the topic of *providence*. They will want to look the word up in Bible dictionaries and theological dictionaries. Alert them that *providence* may seem at first to be a difficult, even abstract concept. Ask them to work out an operating definition for themselves based on their research. Then they should reflect on how Genesis 45:7-8 expresses a concept of *providence*.
- Allow time for persons to share and discuss their findings and reflections.
- Discuss:

—What do you understand by the concept of providence?

—How do you see providence at work in the story of Joseph?

—How do you see providence at work in other stories you have studied in Genesis?
—What do you think about the role of providence in the world today?
—In what ways, if any, have you experienced providence in your own life?
—On a scale from one to ten, with ten being the highest, to what degree do you think providence is a significant force in the world today? in your life?
—How do you see providence at work in the great events of history?

(G) Watch the reversals.

- Read or summarize the information found in the section, "Reversal of Fortunes," pages 109–110 in the study book.
- Ask class members to call out examples in the story of Joseph where a reversal took place. Several such reversals are mentioned in the section, "Reversal of Fortunes."
- Discuss:
—What other reversals of fortunes can you name from other Bible stories you have studied in the Book of Genesis?
—To what extent do you believe that God favors the "underdog" today?
—In what ways does God act today in order to raise up persons who are otherwise weak or without status?
—What other signs have you seen of reversal of fortunes within persons' lives or human history?
—If your personal fortunes were to be reversed today by God, would that reversal be something good or bad for you personally?
—Why do you think God might favor the "underdog"?
—If God favors the "underdog," what do you think should be your stance or response toward that "underdog"?
—In what ways might your stance or response toward an "underdog" be different as an individual from how it would be as a class or as a congregation?
—Who are the "underdogs" today? In what ways should their fortunes be reversed?

Additional Bible Helps

One Last "Meanwhile . . ."
Most of the chapters in the study book contain a sidebar entitled, "Meanwhile . . ." These sidebars were included in recognition of the fact that a thirteen-session study of the Book of Genesis simply could not cover every chapter and verse. These sidebars attempted to fill in the gaps in the Genesis stories by providing a thumbnail sketch of the material not covered in the assigned Bible passages.

At the end of the Bible passages assigned for this session, Joseph's half brothers have just returned to Canaan from Egypt and have announced to Jacob that Joseph is still alive. Jacob's [Israel's] words as Chapter 45 closes are "Enough! My son Joseph is still alive. I must go and see him before I die."

In a sense, the chapters that follow are anticlimactic. By the end of Chapter 45, the problems caused by the hatred the half brothers had felt toward Joseph have now been resolved. Joseph not only stands at the pinnacle of power in spite of having once been sold into slavery, but he has also regained his family. God has acted in such a way to ensure that God's chosen people will survive a terrible famine. God's chosen people are also in a position to suffer enslavement some centuries later in Egypt and thus be in place to be liberated by God in the Exodus.

As Chapter 46 opens, Jacob offers sacrifices to God prior to setting forth on his own journey to be reunited with Joseph in Egypt. God appears one last time in a vision to Jacob, telling Jacob that God will bless the journey to Egypt and will continue to be with Jacob there.

Genesis 46:8-27 provides a summary list of Jacob's descendants.

Genesis 46:28 begins a section telling about the settlement in Egypt of Jacob and his sons. Joseph clears the way with Pharaoh for them to settle as shepherds for Pharaoh in the region of Egypt known as Goshen, which is a fertile, northern border region not far from the routes toward Canaan. In Genesis 47:7-12, Jacob meets and blesses Pharaoh, before the family actually settles in Goshen.

Genesis 47:13-26 describes the rather oppressive food for livestock and land program that Joseph institutes throughout Egypt. If starving Egyptians have no money left, they can simply trade their livestock or their land to Pharaoh in exchange for the food they need in order to survive. "So Joseph bought all the land of Egypt for Pharaoh. All the Egyptians sold their fields, because the famine was severe upon them; and the land became Pharaoh's. As for the people, he made slaves of them from one end of Egypt to the other" (Genesis 47:20-21).

At the end of Chapter 47, a dying Jacob calls Joseph to him to swear that he will not permit Jacob to be buried in Egypt but rather in Canaan, the land of his ancestors.

In Chapter 48, Jacob adopts Joseph's two sons as his own, thus giving his grandsons an equal place in his family as that of their uncles, Joseph's half brothers. Jacob then proceeds to bless the two children. In a curious passage in verses 17-22, Jacob reverses the blessings given to Joseph's two sons, Manasseh and Ephraim, so that the younger Ephraim receives a greater blessing than his older brother. Perhaps in part Jacob recalled how in his youth he contrived to receive a greater blessing than his older brother received.

Chapter 49 sets forth the blessings of the dying Jacob upon his twelve sons. These blessings are presented in poetic form, and forecast the situations that the tribes descended from those sons and bearing their names will encounter later in Israel's history.

In Chapter 50, Joseph oversees the burial of Jacob in Canaan. After the funeral, Joseph's half brothers fear that Joseph will now settle accounts with them. Joseph seeks to reassure them: "Even though you intended to do harm to me, God intended it for good, in order to preserve a numerous people, as he is doing today. So have no fear; I myself will provide for you and your little ones" (verses 20-21).

As the Book of Genesis closes at the end of Chapter 50, Joseph dies at the age of one hundred ten years, is embalmed, and is placed in a coffin in Egypt. The sidebar, "Joseph's Bones," on page 106 of the study book, tells what happened to Joseph's remains centuries later.

How to Create Excitement for Bible Study

by Debra and Gary Ball-Kilbourne

Acts 8:26-40 tells the story of Philip and the Ethiopian eunuch. The eunuch was reading the words of the prophet Isaiah while riding in a chariot. Philip approached him and asked, " 'Do you understand what you are reading?' He replied, 'How can I, unless someone guides me?' And he invited Philip to get in and sit beside him" (Acts 8:30-31).

Philip may not have realized it, but he was teaching a one-person Bible class at that point. How effective was Philip as a teacher? The Bible tells us that the Ethiopian became so excited by what he was taught that he asked to be baptized on the spot.

How can we instill even a fraction of that kind of excitement in the Bible classes we teach?

Too many adult Bible classes follow the same pattern Sunday after Sunday. Standing in front of the class members, the teacher lectures on the Bible text for that week. Attempts at discussion fall flat. The class members continue to attend, perhaps out of a sense of obligation, loyalty, or the need for fellowship. But are they truly being fed from the rich feast of the Scriptures?

What can be done to spice up such an adult Bible class? Three steps can lead your class members into a freshly exciting encounter with God through the words of the Bible: 1) Do your homework. 2) Share your excitement. 3) Risk leading your class members into creativity.

Do Your Homework.
No substitute exists for solid preparation of the material you will teach. To do your homework means to spend time studying the material and developing your lesson before Saturday night.

Take the time to read through the material. Read the Bible text several times. If you usually read the New Revised Standard Version of the Bible, read two or more additional versions. *The New Jerusalem Bible*, *The Revised English Bible*, and the *Good News Bible* would be good choices. Reading these can help you see the different variations in meaning given to the text by translators. Make notes of points or words about which you have questions or that you think are significant.

Consider the following questions:
1. Who wrote the text?
2. When and where was it written?
3. For what audience was it written?
4. Why was it written?
5. What points of contact do your class members have with the situations and needs of the persons who first heard or read the Bible passage you are studying?

Doing your homework will be hard work at times. But it will enrich you *and* the people you teach. Two excellent resources for helping you learn how to study the Bible are *Get Acquainted With Your Bible*, by Gary L. Ball-Kilbourne (Abingdon, 1993) or *Church Bible Study Handbook*, by Robin Maas (Abingdon, 1982).

Share Your Excitement.
If you act bored or indifferent, your class members will too. Suppose you go looking for a new car at a local automobile dealership. The salesperson seems uninterested in selling a car to you. He or she mumbles a few of the facts and figures about the model, shrugs his or her shoulders at your questions, yawns, and looks pointedly at the clock.

Would you really want to buy a car from a salesperson who is not excited about it?

In much the same way you will have a difficult time getting your class members excited about studying the Bible if you are not excited about it. Indeed, if excitement about the good news of Jesus had not crept into Philip's explanation of the Scriptures, the Holy Spirit would probably have found it quite difficult to convert the Ethiopian.

Be enthusiastic as you teach. Let your class members see in your own spirit how God's Spirit filled you with life when you studied the Bible text. Tell them about the struggles you may have had in attempting to understand the difficult parts. Celebrate new insights. Move around. Get excited!

Risk Leading Your Class Members Into Creativity.
The McDonald's Corporation established an innovative policy several years ago in an attempt to foster creativity in its executives. Top managers of the corporation were encouraged to spend some time each week looking through a skylight in the ceiling while resting on a waterbed in a quiet setting. The reason? Meditation in such a setting led McDonald's executives to dream up creative, fresh, and potentially rewarding marketing techniques. McDonald's profitable decision to serve breakfast was, in part, a result of this "waterbed" policy.

When was the last time you spent quality time reflecting about the class you lead and dreaming about how it might be improved?

One important goal of teaching is to help class members convert the material taught into knowledge they can apply to their daily lives. The lecture method is less effective in doing this than other approaches that require greater participation by the class members. Yet, many teachers continue to lecture week after week for fear of trying new teaching methods.

The Adult Bible Class of Riverdale Community Church was studying the Nativity stories one Advent. As teachers of the class, we had done our homework. We had gained several new insights into the Bible texts, especially through reading Raymond E. Brown's *The Birth of the Messiah: A Commentary on the Infancy Narratives of Matthew and Luke* (Doubleday, 1993). We were excited about what we had learned. But how could we share our excitement and knowledge with the class members?

Taking a deep breath, we decided to try an innovative approach. At several locations in the classroom we arranged chairs in a circle. We called each of these circles a "learning center." We then divided the class members into small groups of persons and asked each group to move to a learning center to carry out a specific assignment.

At one learning center we asked persons to read Matthew 2 and Luke 1:5–2:20 and note the differences and similarities in these two accounts of Jesus' birth. In another center we asked the class members to examine the ways familiar Christmas carols celebrate the Nativity and refer to Jesus. In the third learning center we invited class members to create birth announcement cards that would express their feelings about Jesus' birth. Persons in the fourth center studied basic information about shepherds in first-century Judea. We asked these class members to think about what it would have been like to be a shepherd in those days. How would it have felt to be despised throughout Jewish society and yet be among the first to hear the good news of Jesus' birth?

Toward the end of the session we came together as a whole class and shared our new learnings with one another. People were bubbling over with excitement about what they had discovered. They had truly found themselves involved, as if for the first time, with the old, familiar well-loved story of Jesus' birth. Some class members had never been aware of the differences between Luke's and Matthew's accounts of the Nativity. Few of the class members had ever tried to put themselves in the shepherds' place. Most persons appreciated the opportunity to express their learnings and feelings in the birth announcement cards they made.

Creative teaching methods abound if you are willing to learn them and risk using them. You might want to try such different and creative ways of involving class members in the Bible text as

1. dramatic readings;
2. poetry writing;
3. map study;
4. word study using concordances and/or Bible dictionaries;
5. art displays depicting a biblical story or character from various points of view.

In some classes members are accustomed to sitting rigidly in straight lines of chairs or pews. Every week the leader attempts to pour information into the class members' minds like water flowing from a faucet into a bucket. In these classes something as simple as asking members to discuss a question in groups of three may create excitement and interest. Perhaps you might want to invite a neighboring church's adult class to study with you one quarter. Doing so might be particularly challenging if the other church is made up primarily of persons with a different ethnic or racial background than yours. The ideas are almost limitless. Spend some "waterbed time" dreaming up exciting, fresh leadership techniques for use with your class.

For further ideas on creative methods to use and adapt, try *Teaching the Bible to Adults and Youth*, by Dick Murray (Abingdon, 1993).

Adapted from "How to Create Excitement for Bible Study," by Debra and Gary Ball-Kilbourne; *Adult Bible Studies Teaching Helps*, SON 1986. Copyright ©1986 by Graded Press. Used by permission.

The Torah: The Books of God's Community

by Gary L. Ball-Kilbourne

"What do these stones mean?" Joshua 4:21

Exactly how to teach the Bible and do it justice in all its richness and complexity is a challenge. However, the Bible itself offers us clues to ways we can teach the whole Bible in a manner faithful to its varied parts.

Bible scholar Walter Brueggemann suggests that the ancient Israelites held different aims when they developed the three main parts of what Christians call the Old Testament—the Law, the Prophets, and the Writings.

With this view in mind, Brueggemann proposes that "church education, both in its modes and its substance, has gone awry precisely because of the failure to hold these three parts of the canon[1] . . . in balance and in tension."[2]

Realizing that *different parts* of the Bible have *different purposes* requiring *different strategies* can help Christian educators teach the whole Bible today.

The Old Testament itself came into being in order to instruct new generations in the faith of Israel. Its intent in teaching about God is to provide the people with the necessary resources for survival and faithfulness.

Nature of the Torah
The first of the Old Testament canon's three major sections—the Law or the Torah—is primarily made up by the first five books of the Old Testament. It teaches the people of God their unique identity as God's specially gathered community.

● The Torah lays out in no uncertain terms who the people are (God's chosen covenantal people), why they are (God has brought them out of slavery in Egypt to the Promised Land), and how they are expected to live (according to the Ten Commandments plus various rituals, requirements, and prohibitions). The elders of the community teach the children these things so that each new generation will live in a world—God's world—which makes sense, unlike the world of chaos and death characterized by the nations around Israel.

● The Torah is the normative memory of the people—the one basic source they go to in order to recall how they have been made a people by God. That memory is shared by means of stories: the promises made to Abraham and Sarah, of Moses leading the slaves out of Egypt, God's care even when the people rebelled in the wilderness, the giving of the Law at Mt. Sinai, the battles won under Joshua's command.

All these stories define the character of Israel. More importantly, they also define the character of God as perceived by Israel. Nothing else is of such basic value.

Therefore, the stories making up the Torah constitute the norms for life as the people of God. They permit the living of a life that distinguishes Israel from the Egyptians or the Canaanites.

● The Torah comes to Israel by way of revelation—God's actions and promises reveal God's character as one of holiness and righteousness. God's people are likewise to be holy and righteous.

● Accordingly, much of the Torah is made up of laws—rules that help provide the people with the way to be holy as God is holy. The one dominating command above all others is the one against placing other gods before the one God—against idolatry. God is always the central focus of

Timeline for Events of Genesis and Beyond

1. Many of the stories told in the Book of Genesis cannot accurately be assigned any dates within recorded history. Therefore this timeline begins with Abraham.
2. Old Testament events are customarily assigned dates in the era labeled "before Christ" or B.C. Some modern biblical scholars, out of respect for persons who are not Christian, use the term "before the common era" or "B.C.E." Keep in mind that years B.C. count backward.

Date B.C.	The Hebrews	Egypt	Others
2501–2001	Abraham leaves Ur in Chaldea: c. 2100.	Sakkar pyramids built.	
2000–1501	Abraham fathers Ishmael by Hagar, Isaac by Sarah, six children by Keturah. Isaac fathers Esau and Jacob by Rebekah. Jacob fathers twelve sons, including Joseph. Joseph goes into Egypt; saves Egypt from famine; fathers Manasseh and Ephraim by Asenath. Jacob and sons migrate to Egypt.	Hyksos rule, c. 1700–1570. Reign of Amosis I commences. Amenhotep I: 1555–1530. Thutmose I: 1530–1515.	Hammurabi reunites kingdom after overthrow of Babylon by Hittites.
1500–1250	Hebrews in bondage in Egypt under Seti I and Rameses II.	Thutmose III (1480–1450) extends Egyptian empire. Seti I: 1308–1290. Rameses II: 1290–1224–Pharaoh of the Exodus.	Upanishad tradition in India. Dominance of Phoenicians in Mediterranean area.
c. 1250	Moses leads Hebrews from Egypt.		c. 1220–the Trojan War.

the life of the people, and God is always to be the focus of education. Only by remembering God before all else can the people be holy in the sense of being something that is set apart in dedication to God.

- The Torah forces us to realize that some norms are necessary for ordering and preserving human life in a world otherwise filled with chaos. In other words, it provides the people with ethics.

The Greek word from which comes our English word *ethics* literally means "stable"—both in the sense of an animal stall and in the sense of providing security. Developing this image of "stable," the Torah then is God's gift to God's people to provide them with shelter and stability against the chaotic forces of existence.[3]

• The Torah's stories provide identity; its laws offer holiness. Through the Torah, the Bible presents the rock-steady foundation for the grounding of life. Through the Torah, we find ourselves defined as God's community. God has made us a people—God's own people. God has promised to be our God.

This is to be the primary fact that demands to be taught to successive generations in the spirit of both authority and nurture. This fact is our most basic and treasured conviction. We rejoice in sharing it with our children and pray that they in turn will share it with the generations beyond.

Dangers to Watch For
We confront three dangers in teaching the Torah.

• There is the danger that the Torah will become trivial and superficial if its commandments are viewed legalistically. There are commandments to be accepted without debate, but the laws are given (for they are indeed a gift) to be an aid, not a burden. They tell us of the truth about God's ordering of life in this world.

• There is the danger of teaching the Torah in such a way that what we are really presenting as religion are only the values of our culture. Cultural values and aspirations are not religion. In fact, they constantly stand under the judgment of God lest anything be set up as an idol in God's place.

• There is the danger of teaching only the Torah and neglecting the other great sections of the Bible. If we look to only the Law for guidance and if we teach it only for the purpose of indoctrination, we do not teach the whole Bible; and those we teach might never perceive the whole majesty of God. This last danger is avoided as we learn from the other parts of the biblical canon as well as from the Torah.

Story as Primary Method
The way in which the Israelites taught the Torah is just as important as the content of the Law itself. As Brueggemann notes, "the primal mode of education in the church, derived from the Torah, is story."[4]

We can learn from the ways in which the stories found in the Torah are told. They are concrete. They are intended to appeal to the hearers' imaginations. They are told by persons who have experienced them, not by neutral or uncommitted third parties. They are told without the need for further explanation.[5] And they allow the flexibility of memory in their retelling.

A retired pastor once modeled for me a way of teaching the Torah properly—and he did it in his marvelous children's sermons. Rather than use some elaborate object lesson, Glenn would simply tell the children a story—usually one about a child living during Bible times and witnessing some great event we know from the Bible. Very imaginatively, vividly, and simply, Glenn would share the story. Then at its conclusion he would simply stop, saying, "End of story!" He never went on to draw out a point about faith or morality. The *story* was far more important for the children to hear than any "lesson" could be.

Implications for Teaching
What are the implications of the Torah's content and method for Christian education today? For one thing, we realize that we are to make the biblical stories of God's mighty acts and promises our own story. We cannot doubt God's faithfulness to us; it is a given reality we can only accept without question. This is truth, and we must hand it on.

We hand this truth on as we retell the stories about God and God's might among the people.

The issue becomes one of seeing and telling the stories of that which defines us today as the people of God. We might not place much emphasis on Old Testament rituals or on the origin of the twelve tribes, but the stories of God's promises remain the central focus of our life of faith together. Let us, too, find ways to tell their stories in our teaching.

---

[1] *Canon* is the technical term used to talk about the definitive, authoritative collection of the books that make up the Bible. Protestant Christianity accepts thirty-nine books in the Old Testament and twenty-seven books in the New Testament as canon. For more detail about how the canon came about, see the articles included in *The Interpreter's Dictionary of the Bible*, 5 volumes (Abingdon Press, 1962–76).

[2] From *The Creative Word: Canon as a Model for Biblical Education*, by Walter Brueggemann (Augsburg Fortress, 1982), page 11. Readers are urged to read Brueggemann's book for themselves.

[3] For more information see *Ethics in a Christian Context*, by Paul L. Lehmann (Harper and Row, 1963), pages 23–25.

[4] From *The Creative Word*, page 22.

[5] From *The Creative Word*, pages 23–27.

Adapted from "The Torah: The Books of God's Community," by Gary L. Ball-Kilbourne; *Church School Today*, Spring, 1986. Copyright © 1985 by Graded Press. Used by permission.

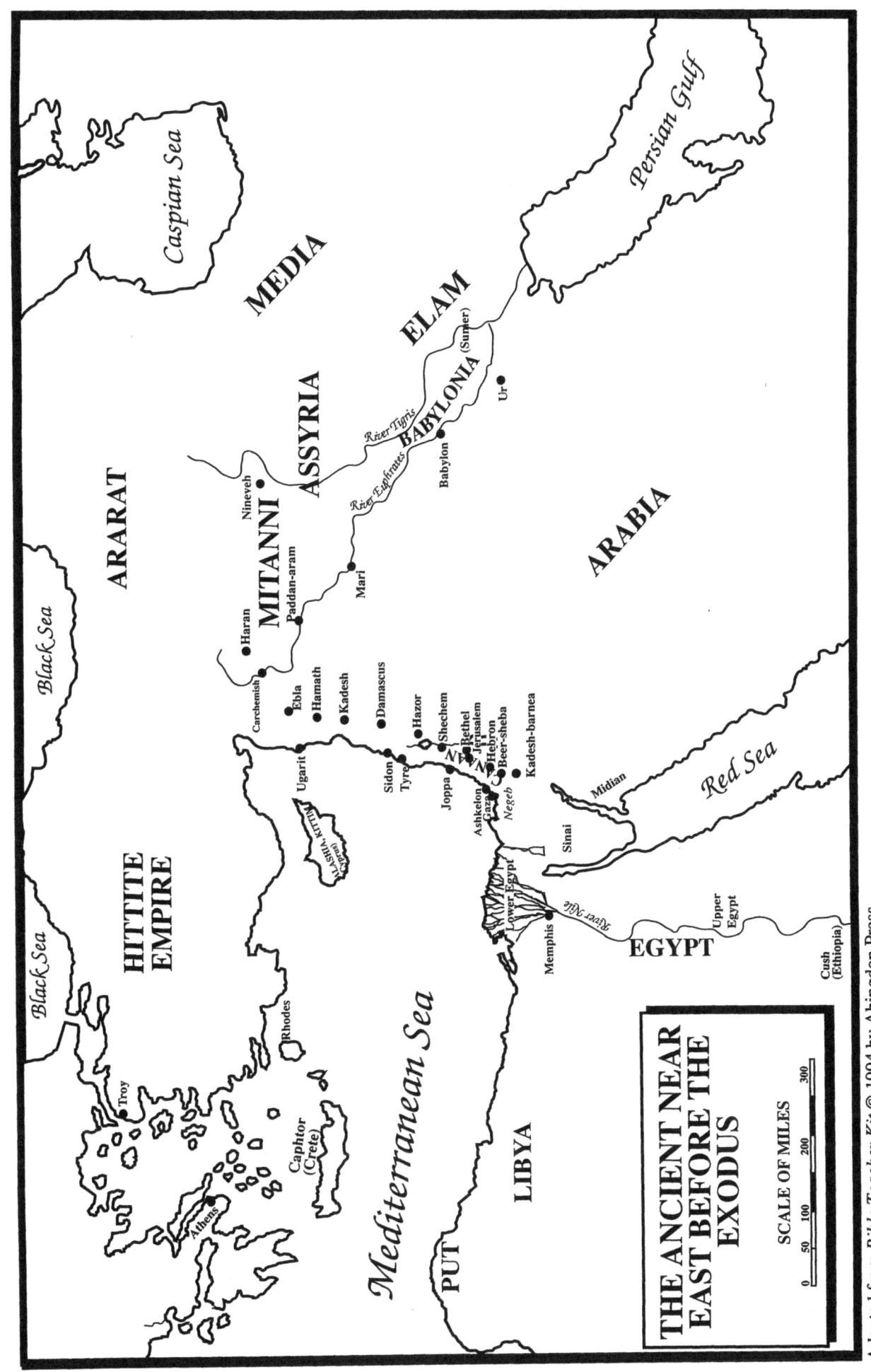

www.ingramcontent.com/pod-product-compliance
Lightning Source LLC
LaVergne TN
LVHW061315060426
835507LV00019B/2171